This Volume is dedicated to Romeo, my education opossum. Romeo was a trouper and he is the opossum in our logo. He taught me perserverance!

CONTENTS

Romeo

INTRODUCTION TO THIS SERIES

Volume 2 deals with many of the diseases and parasites that wildlife may come with into your home or center. We will talk about what causes the disease, treatment options, things you can do. As well as stress, pain management, vaccination, and euthanasia. I will be doing another volume on wound care because that is such a big topic!

Volume 1 and is geared to giving you a comprehensive overview of wildlife rehabilitation including the business side of things, skills, and training, supplies you need, and learning the basics on administering fluids, transportation, triage, warmth, and so much more.

Volume 3 (coming August 2023) will break down individual species, give a treatment plan, feeding schedule, and what specific needs they may have.

My wildlife rehabilitation and conservation career and experience have taken place in the USA. I will talk about my experiences from that perspective. If you are in another country what's a common disease or animal for me may not be as common for you. My experience is predominantly with mammals and turtles.

Disclosure - Volume 2 is meant to help you recognize and treat common problems that present themselves with animals in your care. It should in no way replace advice given by your veterinarian. We assume that you are working with your veterinarian to provide the best possible outcomes.

It is very important to have a good working relationship with your veterinarian. Some states even require that your vet sign off on your paperwork in order to show medical commitment.

Finding a vet that will see wildlife can be tricky. Not all vets will see wildlife or exotic animals in their practice. Furthermore, while some vets will give a discount, vet care can easily be your highest expense.

Some medical procedures you can do yourself and your vet may be willing to give you some training to address common but minor conditions. Things such as giving fluids, administering over the counter meds, vaccinations, and doing a fecal are all easy and necessary skills.

However, such things as X-rays, setting a bone, repairing a severely crushed turtle shell, stitches, or performing an amputation requires a veterinarian. Get prices from your vet upfront.

More importantly dosages should come from your vet because they know more about the situation and wildlife medicine is not a cut and dry science. Ron Hines DVM, a wildlife vet says "veterinary drug dose suggestions for wildlife fly by the seat of their pants".

If you have a small budget for your business, then I suggest that you screen what animals you are able to accept. Taking in orphans who need fluids and then formula feeding until release will cost less than accepting a fawn that has a broken leg because it was hit by a car. These are hard but necessary decisions!

Read Volume 1 Getting Started In Wildlife Rehabilitation, to help you see yourself as a business and stay afloat financially.

Dr. Glaza giving an exam to Ponyo an education groundhog. Photo credit: Ame Vanorio

Learning Skills

There are many ways to learn skills that you can apply to saving wildlife. For me learning is a constant.

- For those of you that are just getting licensed the International Wildlife Rehabilitation Basics course has a lab component.
- Taking classes and going to conferences such as the National Wildlife Rehabilitators will help you gain skills and confidence in how to treat problems.
- I took 16 credit hours in Veterinary Technology course work to gain skills and because I was working for a veterinarian at the time. You may not be as nerdy as I am!
- The online version of MSD (Merck) has 91 quizzes that anyone can take to test their knowledge.
- Find an established rehabber and ask if they will mentor you. You can also begin your career volunteering at a center near you.
- I volunteered at the Cincinnati Zoo to earn some "bird hours" and learned some new skills on treating them.
- Take an online course to gain skills. IWRC has online courses in pain management and
- Check out my YouTube Channel for a couple videos on wildlife rehabilitation. @foxruneec

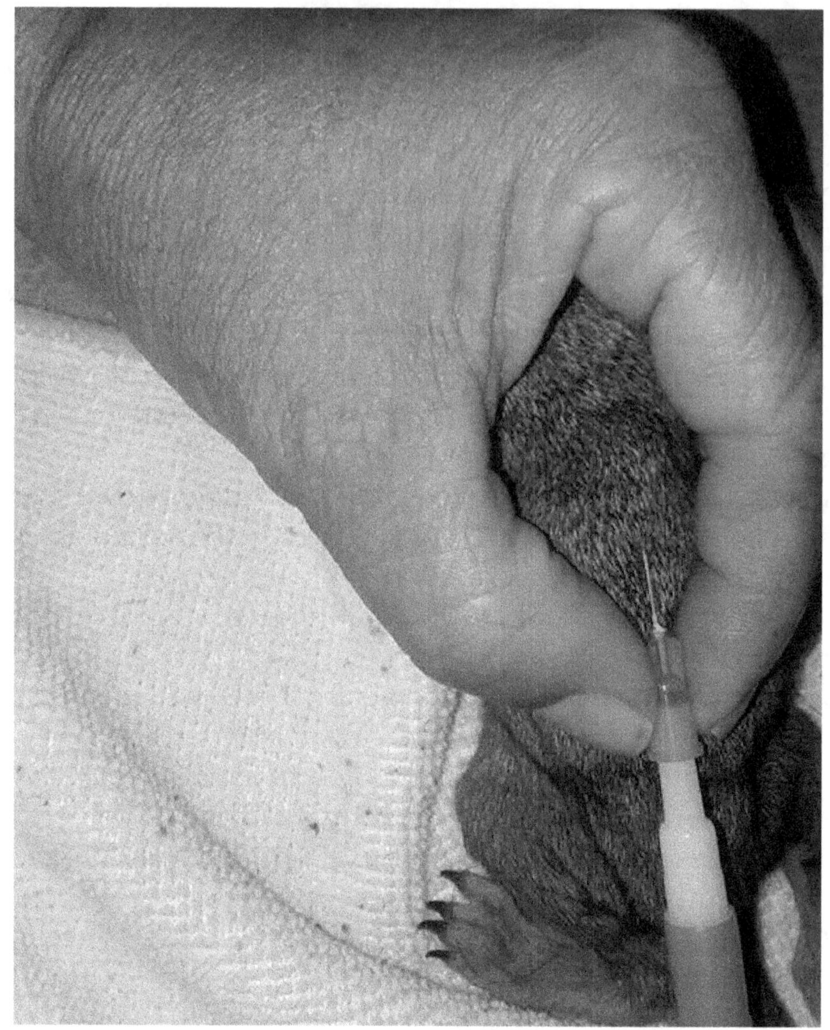

Giving Fluids to a young grey squirrel.

OFF LABEL USE

Medical drugs and treatments are not tested for wildlife use. Except in rare cases testing drugs for wildlife is considered a waste of money by the pharmaceutical industry.

It was interesting during COVID that we were seeing some testing of coronavirus vaccines to be used on endangered animals. However, for the most part we use drugs off-label which means we use it for a different purpose than what is intended for by the US FDA.

Use caution and know that you may have different results than expected. I believe that I once indirectly caused the death of a fawn by giving it a common livestock drug called ivermectin. I went into complete panic and despair. Ivermectin is said to be commonly used on fawns. I had read in wildlife rehabilitators books that ivermectin was a common use drug for deer.

My own vet didn't have a lot of experience with wildlife when we started this journey and was also going by what is published. However, much of what is published may be comparisons with livestock and wildlife. Not actual medical studies on wildlife.

I called a large wildlife facility in Western Kentucky who had a skilled wildlife veterinarian on staff. Dr. Mike, who has since retired, had many years of wildlife experience. He told me that he had noted that fawns were sensitive to ivermectin and gave us suggestions on other treatment plans. Not every vet is going to give free helpful advice, but he was an exception!

Zoonotic diseases or zoonoses are diseases that can be transferred from animal to human or from human to animal. As wildlife rehabilitators we need to be aware of them as many are potentially dangerous.

They can be transmitted via viruses, bacteria, parasites, or fungi. According To Merck pg. 2414 "Wildlife is increasingly recognized as a reservoir for zoonoses including some that were thought to be strictly livestock pathogens" What does that mean for you?

WHAT ARE ZOONOTIC DISEASES?

Rabies is probably the most famous zoonotic disease. The Bubonic Plague was given stardom during the Middle Ages and is still with us today. Others include Salmonella, Leptospirosis, and Roundworms. These diseases come in the form of bacteria, parasites, and viruses.

Interestingly there is also a reverse zoonotic disease where humans can make their pets ill. Examples of this are Staphylococcus aureus (MRSA), H1N1 influenza, and the more recently coronavirus. In 2020 coronavirus was passed from zookeepers to animals in their charge most notable tigers at the Bronx Zoo.

Zoonotic diseases are a public health concern that affects everyone in the community. European countries have been much more proactive in this area than we have been here in the USA. In part possibly because their communities are much older and established with a high incidence of urban wildlife.

Vaccination of wildlife in rehabilitation centers, as well as vaccination programs aimed towards wildlife in public parks and urban areas, has helped to reduce the occurrence of many zoonotic diseases.

Roald, one of my fox releases. Photo credit: Ame Vanorio

In fact, rabies among foxes has been nearly eliminated in thirteen European countries, where it is not unusual to have foxes living in urban areas. Regular vaccination campaigns, often conducted by public health agencies and wildlife conservation organizations, have proven highly effective in reducing the prevalence of the disease in foxes.

In countries such as France, Germany, and Poland, the distribution of bait containing the oral rabies vaccine has been instrumental in immunizing foxes effectively. By enticing foxes to consume the bait, immunization occurs without requiring direct capture or handling of the animals, making it a practical and cost-effective method of disease control.

Wildlife rehabilitators increasingly work with public health officials.

Some zoonotic diseases you may encounter. We will talk about them in more detail in the diseases chapter of the book.

1. Hantavirus: This virus is spread through contact with infected rodent droppings, urine, or saliva. It can cause severe respiratory illness in humans.

2. Lyme disease: This bacterial infection is transmitted to humans through the bite of an infected tick. The disease can cause a range of symptoms, including fever, headache, and joint pain.

3. Rabies: This viral disease is transmitted through the saliva of infected animals, typically through a bite. It can cause severe neurological symptoms in humans and is often fatal if not treated promptly.

4. West Nile virus: This virus is transmitted to humans through the bite of an infected mosquito. It can cause flu-like symptoms and, in severe cases, can lead to neurological damage or death.

5. Tularemia: This bacterial infection is commonly found in rodents, rabbits, and other small mammals. It can be transmitted to humans through contact with infected animals or their fleas, ticks, or insects. The disease can cause fever, skin ulcers, and other symptoms.

6. Plague: Yes, the same thing that killed millions in the Middle Ages can still causes serious illness (except now we are more knowledgeable about treatment) This bacterial infection is most associated with rats and other rodents. It can be transmitted to humans via fleas.

EXTERNAL PARASITES

L et's start by looking at external parasites – the ones you can often see. These critters live on the outside of the animal's body. You may see their eggs, fecal matter, or bodies during an exam. These external parasites are often seen on baby wildlife that come into your rehabilitation center.

The good thing about external pests is that you can often see and identify the adult quite easily. Nymphs and larval stages are very small and may need magnification to identify. Treatments are often easy to apply and purchase.

The challenge with external pests is that they are prolific, and it may take repeated treatments to get them under control. Ticks and fleas have both been found in Antarctica where they feed on northern birds such as penguins. Also, if you are not careful and diligent, they can easily spread throughout your center or your home.

While not related fleas, lice, maggots (flies), mange, and ticks are all animals that suck blood from a host. During feeding, they can spread diseases from pathogens that live in their bodies.

Orphaned baby wildlife is prone to parasites because they have not had a mother to groom them. A heavy load of external parasites may result in anemia, weakness, and secondary skin infections.

Parasites carry many zoonotic diseases, so care must be taken to remove them from the baby while not letting them spread to other animals or humans.

Lyme disease and Rocky Mountain Spotted Fever are two well-known zoonotic diseases that are spread by ticks that also affect humans.

Stocking You Medicine Cabinet

In Volume 1, I talk extensively about preparation and fundraising. Check out that volume to learn more.

Treatments for external parasites can get quite expensive. Put them on your Amazon Wishlist and let your followers know the need.

You should be stocking up BEFORE intake. Make a list of medicines you will need both over the counter and via prescription. Explain to your followers what you need and why you need it.

For example, put this on social media or an email newsletter:

Hello Friends and Wildlife Lovers! Today we are stocking up on Pyrantel Pamoate. We go through a lot of this every season. (insert cute animal picture) Imagine your wild mom is gone, you're hungry and your insides hurt because thousands of roundworms are living in your intestines sucking your blood. Gross! If you are able, please order us a bottle of Pyrantel Pamoate today. This wormer can be used on a variety of species to help rid their bodies of tapeworms, hookworms, and roundworms and put them on the road to recovery.

Initial Exam

When you have an animal enter your facility you need to do an initial exam. Part of this exam will cover looking at the skin, especially loose skin around joints and the genital region. Check into the ears, around the eyes, and between fingers or footpads. These are all places external parasites like to hang out.

Take note of where you see parasites and what species they are. Depending on what other issues the animal is experiencing you will make a plan to treat the parasites. Usually, our first step is to stabilize and triage.

Volume 1 covers an initial exam in more detail.

IDENTIFYING THE CULPRIT

Let's look at the variety of common species and then ways to treat and prevent them.

FLEAS

Fleas are smaller than ticks and hop as their mode of locomotion. You may see pepper-like flecks on the skin which are flea feces. The larvae feed on these feces.

There are over 2200 species of fleas. The species often seen is C. felis or cat fleas. They infest more than 50 species of animals including raccoons, opossums, foxes, bobcats, and rabbits.

Fleas can transmit several diseases including murine typhus to humans. They may also transmit tapeworms.

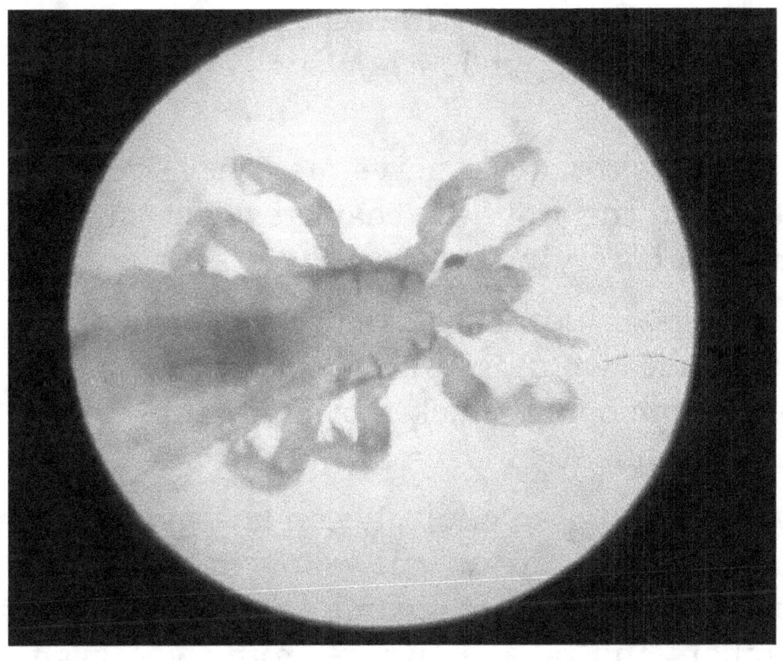

A closeup of a louse

LICE

Lice are very small insects, grey or beige color, with an elongated body. They creep along the skin in between hair follicles or feathers.

Lice are mostly species-specific. So, if baby opossums come in with lice, they typically won't spread to raccoons or squirrels. However, it's best to keep them quarantined and away from other species.

It's worth noting that I rarely had baby possums come in without lice! If you are working with opossums have a delousing plan.

There are two types of lice – bloodsucking which infect mammals and chewing lice which mainly affect birds. You may also see nits, the eggs of the louse. They are sticky and adhere to the hair follicle near the skin.

Maggots

I do not get grossed out easily. I have had vet tech training and assisted my vet during surgeries many times. I have cleaned and sutured wounds. And I've taught in public schools!

But for some reason maggots totally unnerve me! I have vomited giving fawns a bath to clean the wounds. That prevalent smell of decaying flesh combined with a crying baby totally gets me.

Maggots are the larvae stage of flies. Flies like to lay eggs in warm moist places, and this includes wounds. It is common to get a baby animal that has a wound from being attacked by another animal to have maggots. I saw them frequently in fawns.

The fly life cycle moves very fast. An adult fly can lay eggs at only two weeks old. Maggot eggs are white or pale yellow in color. They are frequently in a cluster. The eggs hatch in one to two days. These larvae look like caterpillars and take anywhere from two days to three weeks to get to the next stage which is pupae.

For us the blowfly is of particular concern. The larva of the blowfly actively feeds on living tissue or your baby's body. They need to be removed quickly to keep from damaging the host.

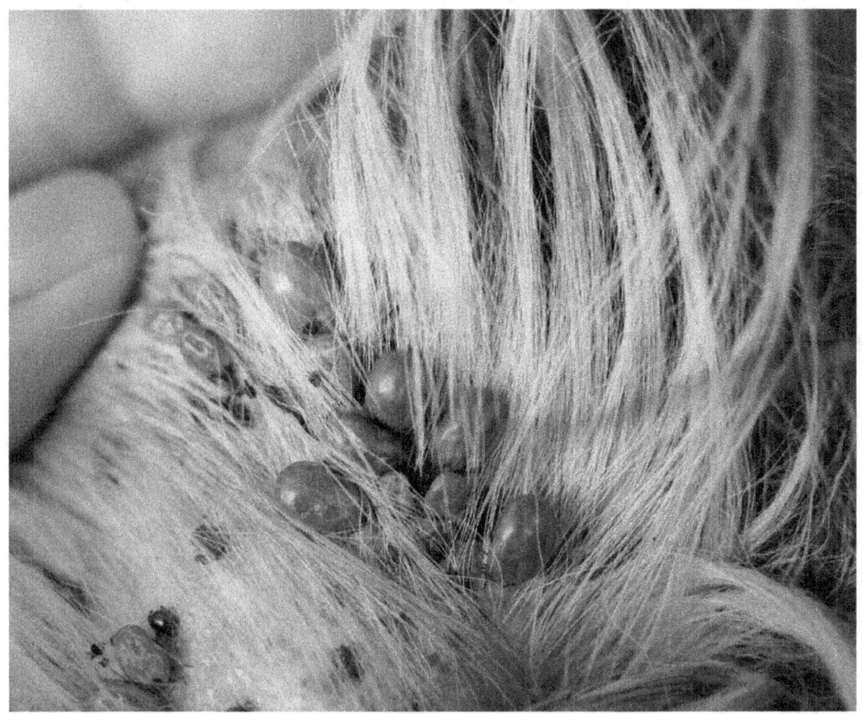

Ticks grouped together in different life stages.

TICKS

Ticks can typically be seen with the naked eye. They may be moving around on the fur or latched on to the skin. Common areas to find them are ears, genitals, belly, in between toes – places where the fur is not thick.

Ticks will infect mammals, birds and even snakes. They are very opportunistic.

Ticks are arachnids and related to spiders. They have four stages in their development – egg, larvae, nymph, and adult. The longer the tick is attached to the host the greater the chance of it transmitting pathogens and toxic saliva.

There are over 850 species of tick that live worldwide with 90 species in North America. The most common are the American dog tick, Brown dog tick, Lone Star tick, Blacklegged tick, and the Rocky

Mountain wood tick. Make sure you know what species live in your location.

There are many products designed to kill ticks. Make sure you are using a product designed and safe for kittens and puppies. Harsh chemicals can harm infant animals. Discuss with your veterinarian what products you should have on hand. (see next section)

*** Keep in mind some wildlife does better with cat prevention and some with dog prevention. Know your species preference.

BEING PREPARED

External parasites are quite common, and you will deal with them on a regular basis. Talk to your vet and have a plan ready. Some treatments you can easily purchase yourself online or locally, and some may need a prescription.

Treatments for external parasites are something I have on hand all year. Stock a variety according to what species you will be rehabbing. Keep reading for some suggestions of things I have used.

REMOVING EXTERNAL PARASITES

Non-chemical ways

- Wear gloves when dealing with parasites.
- Keep incoming animals in a quarantine area away from other animals to avoid transmission.
- Apply insect repellent to your clothes so they don't get on your body and use you as a transportation mode.
- Change bedding frequently. Don't leave infected bedding lying around. Place in a sealed garbage bag to either launder (hot water and high dry) or toss out. For fleas and lice, the Center for Disease Control (CDC) recommends temperatures greater than 128.3 F for ten minutes.
- I also have washed bedding in flea and tick shampoo to assist with destroying any that is on the bedding.
- Ticks and maggots may be easy to pick off by hand. Use tweezers or a special tick removal tool.
- The CDC recommends using tweezers to grab the tick as close to the skin as possible. Pull upwards without twisting. Don't squish the tick because that can spread disease through body fluids.
- Flea and lice combs are also useful to remove them and then dunk in soapy water.
- Fleas can sometimes be removed by using a lint roller or masking tape to catch them.

USING CHEMICAL PRODUCTS

- Products that are made for domestic animals can be used for wildlife. Caution is needed to use the correct dosage and type of treatment per species. Typically, they are different for cats and dogs.
- A bath can be given using an insecticide soap made for kittens or puppies. Use caution because this may cause undue stress to wildlife and cause further compilations.
- For neonate or compromised animals put the powder or spray on a cloth and then gently wipe it on the body. Don't spray chemicals or put topicals on infants.

Here are some of the more common brands. Generic brands are also widely available.

- Fipronil (Frontline) comes in tubes of liquid chemical that is dripped on the animal between the shoulder blades. Frontline also comes in a spray. I sprayed a cloth and then wiped the neonate's body being careful to avoid eyes and mouth. The spray can also be used on reptiles for ticks and mites. Care should be taken to avoid the head. Do not use Fipronil on rabbits.

- Imidacloprid (brand name Advantage) is a popular topical treatment used on pets. It is sold by the weight of the animal and is considered safe for domestic babies over eight weeks. Younger animals may only need a drop or two placed between the shoulder blades. Talk to your vet about dosage.

- Permethrins and pyrethrins are common in sprays and powders that are used on pets, livestock, and gardens to kill insects. They can be applied to a cloth and then to the animals. There are also permethrin products made for reptile use. Use these products on the underside of bedding and make sure animals can not lick it off each other.

- Selemectin (Revolution) is a monthly treatment also designed for domestic pets. It is a prescription and stronger. Used to treat both external and internal parasites on domestic animals. I use this only on healthy juveniles and adults. It also works well on mange but does require several treatments. It requires a prescription or purchase through your vet.

I am all in favor of treating pests naturally as I was a certified organic farmer for many years. However, we need to consider a few things first. The number of parasites on the baby, the size of the liter, and other factors that may be compromising their health.

For compromised wildlife, I start with a chemical treatment and then use a natural treatment for controlling the pests. This is because I need something that will act quickly to help stabilize the health of the animal.

Natural products are great, but they don't often kill the parasite quickly thus eliminating the issue. In some cases, time is essential to save the life of the animal.

DIATOMACEOUS EARTH

Diatomaceous earth is a popular way to treat insects in organic gardening. It was first registered in 1960 to kill garden pests. It's listed for use against ticks, fleas, spiders, and bed bugs.

It's made from tiny aquatic animals called diatoms. These diatoms contain silica which commonly occurs in sand, clay, and quartz. The silica is crushed creating a flour-like powder. This powder can be used in a dry or wet form.

Silica causes the insect to dry out and may puncture their exoskeleton. Animal bedding is typically dusted with the powder form.

Care should be taken not to breathe in the dust or allow it to get in the eyes. Treat the animal's bedding and don't put it directly on a baby.

APPLE CIDER VINEGAR

While it won't kill adult lice, apple cider vinegar will cause the nits protective coating to break down killing these eggs. Then use a lice comb to remove the nits.

Use caution on infants because vinegar is acidic and can irritate the skin. Swab nits with a cotton ball or Q-Tip soaked in apple cider vinegar.

HERBS TO REPEL PESTS

Having herbs in your nursery area can help to repel pests, however, they won't kill them. Herbs in the mint family – oregano, peppermint, and sage – are all good. Cloves is a natural pest repellent.

I have several organic gardening blogs on my website that talk about growing and using medicinal herbs.

Vet's Best is a commercial flea and tick product that uses certified natural oils.

NATURAL POPULATION CONTROL

You can encourage natural parasite predators on your own property and advocate for them in public areas. Many animals eat ticks including birds, opossums, ants, and spiders.

I love to tell people all about tick-eating opossums and wild turkeys. This is a great way to give the public some positive wildlife facts. Opossums especially are often treated inhumanly by humans.

There are several types of mites. Mites are common in ears and under the skin. They are ridiculously small, and some are microscopic.

Mites are arachnids that burrow under the skin. They reproduce rapidly and can also infect bedding and cages. I saw the sarcoptic mange commonly in raccoons and red foxes.

Mites can affect all mammals and even reptiles.

MANGE

The most severe mites that I see are mange. They cause hair loss and skin infections.

Mange causes several symptoms:

- Severe itching
- Skin that is scaly, and irritated looking
- Distinct bad smell from dead skin and infection
- Hair loss especially face, legs and groin
- Severe causes leave crusty lesions on the body
- Swelling especially around eyes

Seborrhea is the veterinary term for thickening of the skin.

Mange is serious. The symptoms can become so bad that the animal can't hunt and begins to starve to death. This is when you will get phone calls. These animals are hungry and start coming into people's yards looking for food or help.

You can check for mites by viewing a skin scraping under a 4X setting on a microscope.

SARCOPTIC

Typically affects bobcat, coyote, fox, rabbit, raccoon, squirrels, and porcupine. The mites typically start around the head and can spread to the entire body in a matter of weeks. By the time you get the report on an animal, they have most likely been infected for several months.

The entire life cycle is spent on the host and lasts about 21 days. It is transmitted by direct contact and the young often get it from the parent.

DEMODEX

Typically affects bears, coyotes, foxes, and opossums. There are several species of this mange according to Merck Veterinary Manual and has been a problem in cattle. These mites live in the hair follicles and sebaceous glands of their hosts.

All life stages can happen on the host which means that they reproduce rapidly. Clinical signs occur anywhere from ten days to eight weeks.

Red fox with severe mange

TREATING MANGE

Treating mange is a commitment and requires several types of medicine. You need to talk to your veterinarian and have a plan for how you will handle mange patients or if you will accept mange patients.

Mange can be expensive because it requires several treatments, and it takes management because you will need housing away from other animals.

It can be hard if you get in a juvenile or adult animal because they really need two doses 2-4 weeks apart. However, as a stressed adult you may decide to just give one dose plus nutritional support and release so not to cause undue stress or habituation.

I have had success with treating adult raccoons and foxes with mange using Selemectin (Revolution). Revolution is a spot-on dose that makes it less invasive and easier to administer. The Merck Veterinary Manual suggests 6mg/kg. The nice thing about the

Revolution is it comes in doses based on size.

In addition, Merck states that two doses of Imidacloprid-Moxidectin, brand name Advantage Multi (prescription), is effective on dogs and cats. Advantage II (non-prescription) is available for ferrets.

With young animals, neonates, and young juveniles, there is a concern because often recommended drugs, Ivermectin and Selemectin are so strong.

I typically give a dose before release to protect the animal from reinfestation. My goal is to release them back in their home territory even though I may know this to be a hot spot for mites. I feel the animal will adjust better and has a better chance of finding food in their home territory.

Dips or baths in solutions such as Mitaban (prescription) also work, however this is not advisable for many wild animals. It causes a great amount of stress, and the animal may become aggressive. One option is to have a vet sedate the animal so you can do a skin treatment but there is a certain amount of stress and risk there as well.

In addition, your vet may decide to give antibiotics and steroids. Antibiotics are needed when the animal has secondary infections usually caused by scratching. Steroids such as prednisone help control the itching so they may start to heal.

CLEAN AND ISOLATE

Mange is very contagious and will spread to other animals in your care. In addition, humans can get mites. They can not reproduce on your body, but they can dig in and chew on your skin. This will cause intense itching and possible pain.

- Keep the animal with mange in isolation.
- Wear gloves when you treat, feed, or clean the mange animal.
- Bedding should be changed daily, placed in a sealed garbage bag, and thrown out.

FUNDING TREATMENT

Mange has a long treatment time of one to two months. The ideal situation is to bring the animal into your clinic. However, it's not always possible to get them trapped and transported.

Consider your funds when caring for an animal with mange. Medicine costs alone can easily top $500. In addition, the animal will need basic care during that time and housing away from other animals.

It has become more acceptable to assist the "finder" with leaving out food containing medicine. When someone calls – typically about a fox in their neighborhood – I ask for a photo. When I identify mange, I give them some information about the parasite and refer them to a vet for more information should they need it.

Skunk baby being examined for pests. Photo credit Ame Vanorio

Once identified with mange and they are willing, I give detailed instructions on the procedure. I have the finder go to an area feed store or online and purchase meds. They can then place the medicine in food and set it out for the animal.

There are several problems with this, and many rehabilitators don't advise finders to try it.

- Another animal may eat the medicated food.
- An animal that is sensitive to the medicine may consume the drug and get sick.
- This practice may be illegal in your state.
- Repeated treatments are needed.
- Wild animals are hard to monitor.

It is my personal belief (hope) that if you can get one dose in them, they will start to feel better and begin to hunt again. Sometimes the animal becomes so infested they just walk into a yard looking for food or help. In this case it may be easy to place medicated food nearby and have the homeowner watch it consumed. Nutrients will help them become stronger and fight off mites.

Hotline For Wildlife has a PDF on this with some good resources that I will link to below.

Now let's move on to the parasites we can't readily see. Internal parasites live inside the body most frequently in the digestive system. We do occasionally see them at the anus or in fur surrounding it.

Doing Fecal Floats

I learned how to do fecal exams when I worked as a vet assistant. It has been a very valuable skill.

A fecal float is simple enough. You take some feces from the animal, mix it with a solution, and examine it under a microscope. There are charts and textbooks to help you learn identification.

Obviously, some equipment needs to be purchased but an adequate microscope can be purchased for around $100, and the slides and floatation solution are relatively inexpensive. The expense is worth it especially when comparing it to the cost of a veterinarian doing it.

Prevention of Worms

Worms will come into your center inside little bodies. You will need to take cautions, so they don't spread to humans or other animals.

Wear gloves and treat bedding as contaminated. Many worm species can infect humans.

Worming Medicines

There are several worming medicines available and some work better than others on certain strains or species. Also, some wormers are quite strong, and care should be taken with young, compromised bodies. One wormer I use is Pyrantel Pamoate Suspension because it is low risk and treats a number of species of parasites.

Hookworms

Hookworms live in the alimentary (digestive) system of mammals. They are widely dispersed with 68 known species and inhabit a range of hosts causing gastrointestinal distress and anemia. In wildlife they are most diverse among bears, bobcats, and red foxes. However, they infect a wide range of mammals including raccoons and skunks.

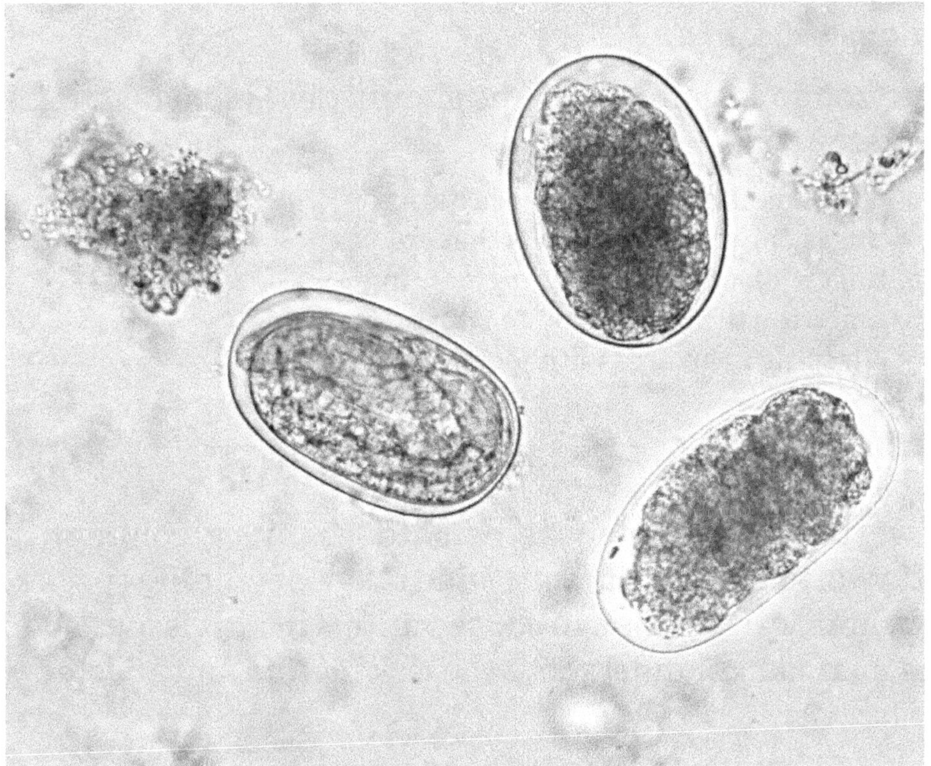

Hookworm eggs

Hookworms feed on the blood of their hosts causing weight loss, diarrhea, and unexplained lethargy.

Symptoms of Hookworms:

- Weight loss
- Diarrhea
- Anemia
- Lethargy
- Respiratory issues
- Not growing
- Skin irritation

Treatment typically involves administering appropriate anthelmintic medications and providing supportive care to enhance the wildlife patient's recovery. To prevent further spread, infected animals are isolated from healthy ones and their enclosures are meticulously cleaned.

They are zoonotic so precautions should always be taken. They can be transferred via:

- From mother to infant via lactation
- Ingesting smaller animals that are
- Ingestion of eggs through grooming
- Entering the body through skin on feet
- Sleeping in an area with feces

Roundworm

Roundworms, also known as nematodes, are a common type of parasitic worm that can infect a wide range of wildlife species. These small, cylindrical worms can cause various health issues in animals, making it crucial to understand the risk factors and affected wildlife species.

Numerous mammals can become hosts for roundworms. Common culprits include raccoons, foxes, coyotes, skunks, and rodents such as mice and rats. Roundworms typically infect these animals through the ingestion of contaminated soil, water, or prey. Infections can have detrimental effects on the overall health and well-being of infected mammals.

Symptoms of Roundworms:

- Bloated abdomen
- Low weight
- Poor coat
- Lethargy
- Diarrhea and/or vomiting
- Observation of worms or ova in feces or at rectum

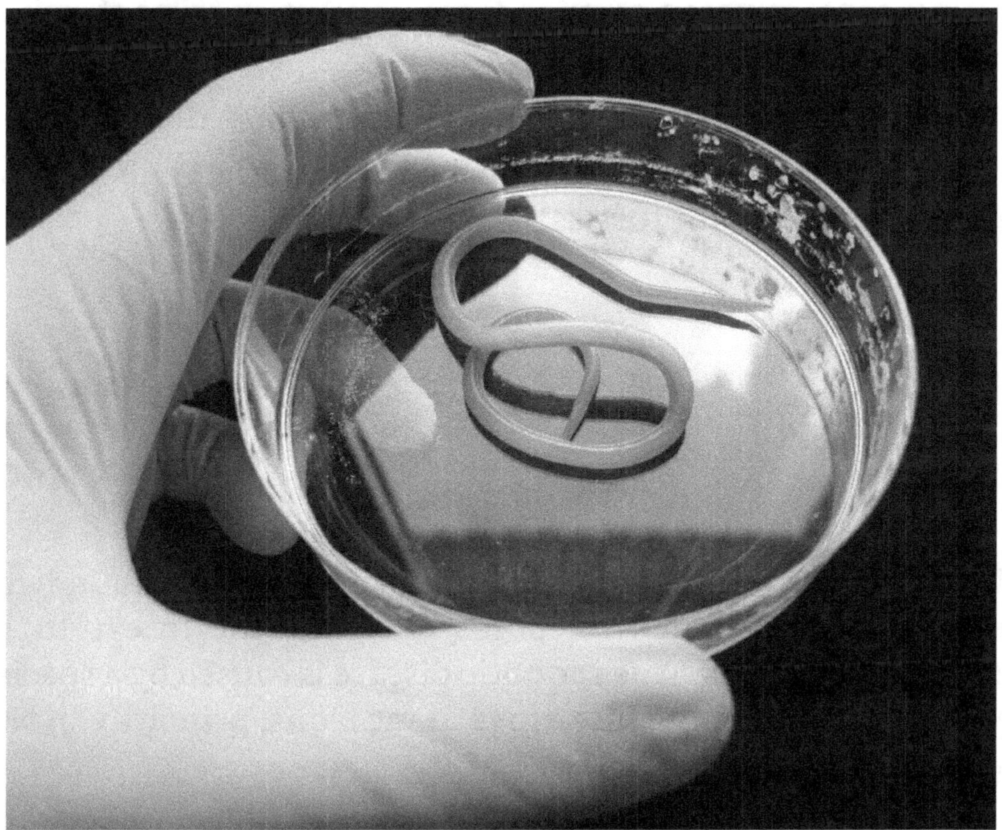

Ascaris nematode, Roundworm

These worms can be identified as spaghetti-like, white or tan in color, and are typically several inches long. However, this symptom may not always be present, especially if the infection is in the early stages.

Avian species can also become susceptible to roundworm infections. Certain bird species, particularly raptors and waterfowl, are prone to infection due to their feeding habits. For example, eagles and hawks may contract roundworms by consuming infected rodents or other small mammals, while waterfowl can become infected through the consumption of contaminated aquatic organisms or plants.

Although less commonly observed, some reptiles can also harbor roundworms. Turtles and snakes are the primary reptilian species susceptible to infection. These animals may become infected by ingesting contaminated prey or from contact with contaminated soil or water.

Due to the hidden nature of these infections, diagnosing and treating roundworms in reptiles can be challenging. Fenbendazole is often recommended for turtles.

Baylisascaris procyonis

Baylisascaris procyonis, commonly known as raccoon roundworm, is a parasitic infection that poses a significant threat to both raccoons and humans. This zoonotic disease is caused by a species of roundworm found in the intestines of raccoons, primarily in North America.

The life cycle of Baylisascaris procyonis begins when raccoons, the definitive host, shed millions of microscopic eggs through their feces. These eggs are highly resilient and can remain infectious in the environment for years. Once ingested by intermediate hosts such as rodents, birds, or other small mammals, the eggs hatch into larvae, which then migrate throughout the body, including the brain.

Raccoons infected with Baylisascaris procyonis may exhibit subtle or no symptoms at all. However, heavy infestations can lead to neurological disorders, including unusual behavior, disorientation, and impaired movement. Additionally, these raccoons may suffer from intestinal blockages and malnutrition. In severe cases, the infection can be fatal.

Pyrantel pamoate can be given. In addition, praziquantel tablets has had good results. Talk to your veterinarian about dosage.

Humans are accidental hosts and can be infected by ingesting infective eggs present in contaminated soil, water, or objects contaminated with raccoon feces. Once the larvae migrate through the human body, they can cause devastating effects, primarily on the central nervous system.

Roundworms are considered a zoonotic disease. Young children are the highest risk so keep this in mind if you have a young family and do rehab. The raccoon roundworm ova can migrate to the eyes and brain in humans causing permanent damage.

In an article by Dr. Sapp her team tested 347 asymptomatic adult wildlife rehabilitators for B. procyonis antibodies; 24 were positive, suggesting that subclinical baylisascariasis is occurring among this population.

Sarah G H Sapp has written several articles about Baylisacaris as it pertains to human health (See Resources)

Tapeworms

Tapeworms are a type of internal parasite that can commonly affect wildlife mammals.

Tapeworms, scientifically known as cestodes, are a type of segmented flatworm that belongs to the class Cestoda. They are parasitic organisms that inhabit the digestive tracts of their hosts. Tapeworms have a unique body structure that consists of a head (scolex), a neck, and numerous segments called proglottids.

Tapeworms have a complex life cycle that typically has numerous hosts. The adult tapeworm resides in the intestines of a definitive host, which in the case of wildlife mammals could be carnivores such as foxes, coyotes, or wildcats. Tapeworm eggs are shed through the feces of the definitive host and can contaminate the environment.

Intermediate hosts, such as small mammals, birds, or even insects, consume tapeworm eggs while foraging. Once inside the intermediate host, the tapeworm eggs hatch, and larvae, known as cysticercoids, develop in various tissues. Predators, including wildlife mammals, become infected with tapeworms by consuming intermediate hosts harboring cysticercoids.

Symptoms of Tapeworms:

- Weight loss
- Poor Coat
- Digestive Disturbance
- Itchy rectal area – animal may scoot on bottom

Identification – the segments look like grains of rice. They can be seen outside the anus and in the feces.

Proglottid, a tapeworm segment.

DISEASES

(Diseases are listed in alphabetical order)

Coccidiosis

If you are a farmer, you are probably familiar with coccidiosis as it's common with baby poultry and ruminants. This disease is caused by microscopic protozoan parasites called coccidia, which inhabit the intestinal tract of the host.

Coccidiosis is highly contagious and spreads through the ingestion of contaminated food or water, or through direct contact with infected animals or their feces. The parasites target the cells lining the intestinal lining, leading to inflammation, diarrhea, weight loss, and decreased productivity.

These are protozoa which live in the intestines and multiply quickly. They may be present in adult animals but typically do not cause issues. A fecal test can detect their presence.

I personally found this to be common in fawns. I'm not sure if this was due to me being in a rural area and the deer being around other ruminants such as cattle and goats but that was my suspicion.

Symptoms:

- Diarrhea – may be watery and contain blood
- Weight loss
- Loss of appetite
- Dehydration – sunken eyes, dry mouth
- Poor growth
- Poor coat or feathers
- Weak
- Abdominal discomfort – hunched over
- Anemic – pale gums

Symptoms can vary depending on the severity of the infection and the animal species affected. Coccidiosis can be prevented through proper hygiene practices, regular deworming, and the use of appropriate medications or vaccines.

Prompt diagnosis and treatment are crucial to control the spread of the disease and minimize its impact on animal health and production.

Corid ® is a popular over the counter livestock brand available on Amazon and in feed stores. Corid may make the body have difficulty processing B1 so consider giving that as a supplement.

Sulfa drugs such as trimethoprim/sulfamethoxazole (generic Bactrim®) are also used on livestock. Animals receiving sulfa drugs must consume extra fluids to prevent crystallizing in their kidneys. "All sulfa drugs have the potential to cause urinary tract "stones" (calculi) when animals are dehydrated and/or do not consume plenty of water" (Hines DVM).

Studies among livestock population have shown that young animals have a high incidence, and it correlates to stressors such as weaning, shipping, and overcrowding.

There is a vaccine available for poultry but not canids.

Distemper

Distemper in wildlife is very common in certain parts of the country. Distemper is a highly contagious viral disease that affects wildlife populations worldwide. It can impact a wide range of species, including raccoons, foxes, skunks, wolves, and coyotes.

I had my center in Kentucky for 12 years and distemper was my biggest disease problem – after dehydration and being hit by a car. It's a very sad situation to see repetitive cases of the disease. Often animals come in when they have reached the advanced stages and exhibiting "lack of fear".

Distemper is caused by the canine distemper virus (CDV), a close relative of the measles virus. It primarily affects the respiratory, gastrointestinal, and central nervous systems of infected animals.

Many times, when finders spot an animal that has Distemper and that has locomotion issues they panic because they assume it's rabies. Distemper can also mimic Rocky Mountain Spotted Fever.

Distemper is transmitted through direct contact with an infected animal or through exposure to contaminated food and water sources. It can be spread through respiratory droplets and through the placenta is pregnant females.

Symptoms:

- Fever
- Nasal and eye discharge
- Sores around eyes
- Coughing
- Vomiting
- Incoordination and locomotion issues including head tilt and circling
- Seizures
- Appears friendly
- "Hard Pads"

One visible manifestation of distemper is the hardening and thickening of the foot pads, causing them to become rough and dry. This phenomenon is known as "hard pad" and is often accompanied by the formation of cracks and sores on the pads. Animals who recover from the disease may continue to exhibit hyperkeratosis or a thickening of the skin (Merck, pg 777)

Another check for distemper is to shine a light on the eye. Bright green eye-shine during daylight is also a symptom.

Some rehabilitators feel they can smell distemper and that it has a distinct foul odor.

There is no cure for canine distemper infection. Treatment typically consists of supportive care such as controlling vomiting, diarrhea and neurologic symptoms; and combat dehydration through administration of fluids. (AVMA)

I personally have seen distemper most in raccoons but have also taken in fox, otter, and mink that tested positive for distemper. Know what species are likely to have it in your area.

While distemper is caused by a different virus, Tamiflu has shown some efficacy in reducing viral replication and relieving symptoms in certain cases. Treating distemper with Tamiflu can be a potential option for managing the symptoms and reducing the severity of the illness. Tamiflu, also known as Oseltamivir, is an antiviral medication commonly used to treat influenza viruses. There have been no conclusive studies on its effects on canids. (Merck, 2748)

As distemper can have varying effects on different animals, it is essential to consult with a veterinarian to determine the most appropriate treatment plan and ensure the best possible outcome for the affected animal.

Distemper spreads through aerosolized respiratory droplets, direct contact with infected individuals, or sharing of contaminated food and water sources. Given that raccoons and foxes are social animals and often interact closely with each other, the virus can spread rapidly within their communities.

Additionally, infected animals shed the virus in their bodily fluids, increasing the risk of transmission to other susceptible species, including domestic dogs.

Karen Bailey of the Kentucky Wildlife Center did a presentation on raccoon distemper at the IWRC conference in 2012. (see resources)

Make sure your domestic dogs are vaccinated!!

Do Distemper Tests for Animals Work?

There are a number of distemper tests on the market that you can purchase and use.

Distemper tests are designed to detect the presence of antibodies or antigens associated with the distemper virus in an animal's body. These tests are typically conducted using blood, urine, or nasal swab samples.

The reliability of distemper tests largely depends on various factors, including the test type, timing, and the animal species being tested. There are two main types of distemper tests: antibody tests and antigen tests.

Antibody tests detect the presence of antibodies produced by the animal's immune system in response to a distemper infection. These tests are commonly used by veterinarians to determine if an animal has been previously exposed to the virus or has received a distemper vaccination. They are generally reliable and accurate, providing valuable information about an animal's immune status.

On the other hand, antigen tests are primarily used to identify active distemper infections. These are the types often used by wildlife rehabilitators to determine if there is an infection.

While antigen tests can be useful in identifying infected animals, their accuracy may vary depending on the test sensitivity, the stage of infection, and the viral load present in the sample. It is important to note that no test is 100% foolproof, and false negatives or positives may occur.

Rehabbers often combine test results with their observations on the animal's health.

Animals in the early stages can be treated with fluids, antibiotics, and anticonvulsants. Care for these cases can get quite expensive and the ability to be released must be considered. In addition, animals who have recovered can shed the virus for up to three months and should remain isolated.

Recovery and successful release of animals with severe cases is low and these animals should be considered for euthanasia.

Prevention is possible with vaccines. There are a variety of vaccines some which may be better for one species over another. Vaccines are modified live and can be given as young as four weeks.

Giardiasis

*** Zoonotic – One species Giardia duodenalis (syn. Giardia lamblia and Giardia intestinalis) affects humans and other mammals

This protozoon affects numerous species although you may hear it referred to as "Beaver Fever". It is often seen in animals who live in or around water such as beavers, minks, otters, and raccoons. They also affect birds, reptiles and amphibians.

The infection is primarily transmitted through the consumption of contaminated food or water, making it a significant concern for those in areas with poor sanitation or inadequate water treatment systems.

Transmitted by ingestion contaminated food and/or water.

The Giardia parasite survives in the environment by forming a protective outer shell, known as a cyst, which allows it to withstand harsh conditions.

Once ingested, these cysts travel to the small intestine, where they release active parasites that attach to the intestinal lining. The parasites then interfere with the absorption of nutrients from food, leading to the characteristic symptoms of giardiasis.

Symptoms:

- Diarrhea
- Abdominal cramps
- Bloating
- Gas
- Dehydration
- Nausea
- Fatigue

Regular fecal examinations should be conducted to identify infected individuals. Fecal Examination: Fecal testing is considered the primary method of diagnosing Giardiasis. Wildlife rehabilitation centers can collect fresh fecal samples from the animals and examine them under a microscope for the presence of Giardia cysts or trophozoites.

Centers may employ flotation techniques, sedimentation techniques, or direct smear methods.

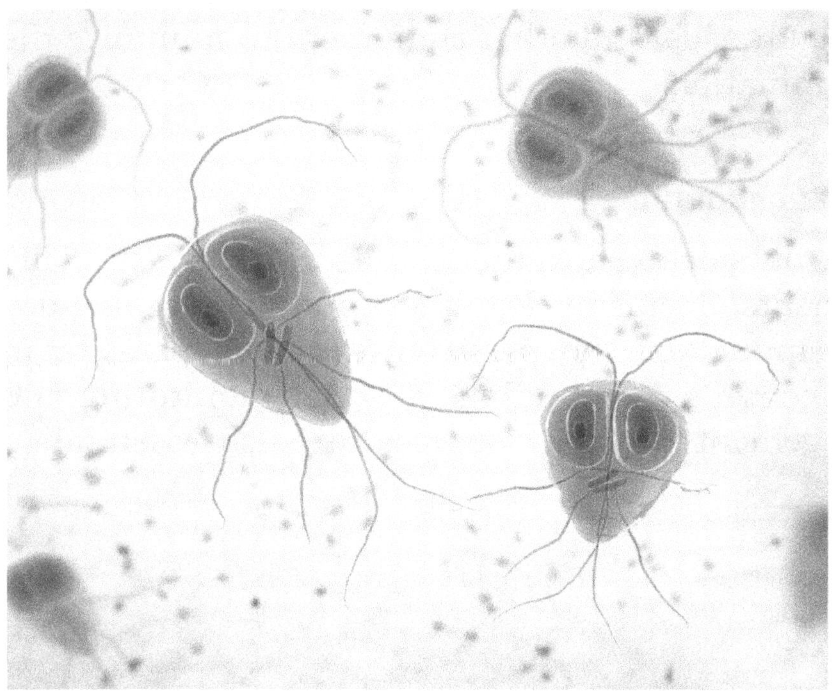

Giardia computer animation – sadly they
look like cute little monsters!

Antigen-based tests involve the detection of specific Giardia proteins in fecal samples. Centers can use enzyme immunoassays (EIAs) or immunochromatographic assays to identify Giardia antigens. These tests are relatively quick and can provide accurate results within a shorter timeframe compared to traditional microscopic examination.

Treatment is often in the form of a wormer. According to Merck, Fenbendazole is the most common one used to kill giardia.

Isolation and hygiene:

Infected animals should be isolated from healthy individuals to prevent the transmission of the parasite. Stringent hygiene practices must be followed, including regular cleaning and disinfection of enclosures, feeding utensils, and other equipment to minimize the risk of cross-contamination.

Environmental management:

Giardia can survive outside the host for extended periods, especially in moist environments. Ensuring cleanliness and maintaining dry enclosures can help reduce the persistence of the parasite in the rehabilitation center's surroundings. Regular monitoring and appropriate management of water sources are also essential to prevent reinfection.

Leptospirosis

***Zoonotic

Leptospirosis, an infectious disease caused by the bacteria Leptospira is known as Weil's disease in humans. This bacterial infection affects both humans and animals, making it a zoonotic disease. There are more than 250 species, and they are often regional or species specific. It thrives in moist areas and is more common in tropical and sub-tropical regions of the world.

The bacteria responsible for leptospirosis are commonly found in soil and water contaminated with the urine of infected animals. Wild animals that are potential reservoirs include raccoons, skunks, squirrels, insectivores (moles, shrews, hedgehogs), opossums, deer, rodents, buffalo, and marsupials.

Symptoms:

- Fever
- Lack of appetite
- Muscle pain
- Chills
- Vomiting

- Blood in urine
- Feces that are black like tar
- Red eyes
- Runny eyes and nose

It is important to note that leptospirosis may be asymptomatic. It can also cause severe organ failure. So, a wide range of effects.

Leptospires can survive in infected carcasses and be transmitted to scavengers. The bacteria invade the body through the gastrointestinal tract, mucous membranes, urogenital system, upper respiratory tract, and eye. Open wounds or skin abrasions can also serve as a point of entry for the bacteria.

The treatment plan for leptospirosis in wildlife typically involves a

combination of antibiotics, like tetracyclines and penicillin, which can help combat the infection. However, the dosage and duration of treatment may vary depending on the severity of the infection and the specific species being treated.

Supportive care, including fluid therapy and nutritional support, is often necessary to aid in the recovery process.

Vaccines against leptospirosis are available for pigs, cattle, and dogs. They are not available for horses or humans.

Additionally, during the rehabilitation process, measures should be taken to prevent the spread of the bacteria to other animals, staff, or visitors. This may involve isolation of infected individuals, the use of personal protective equipment, and thorough disinfection protocols.

Lyme Disease

***Zoonotic disease and can be transferred to humans

Black legged ticks are considered the most common carrier however all ticks can carry the bacteria spirochete which causes Lyme disease. Ticks will attach themselves to mammals, birds, and reptiles.

According to Iowa State dogs and other canids, horses and sometimes cattle can get Lyme disease. White-tailed deer, mice, chipmunks, gray squirrels, opossums and raccoons can also be infected. Remember a neonate without a mother to groom them often becomes infested with ticks.

Some mammals, lizard, and avian species contract the disease but don't have symptoms. For instance, fawns may have multitudes of ticks and are important to the tick as a source of blood. However white-tailed deer very infrequently get Lyme disease.

Deer are often described by scientists as "noncompetent reservoirs". This means they do not efficiently harbor and transmit B. burgdorferi (Pearson, 2022).

Fawn bottle feeding. Photo credit: Ame Vanorio

Symptoms:

- Lameness
- Swollen Joints
- Swollen lymph nodes
- Lethargy
- Weight Loss
- Fever
- Behavioral Changes
- Respiratory Distress
- Skin Abnormalities
- Eye and Ear Inflammation
- Mortality

Many rehabilitators put animals who come in with a heavy load of ticks on a preventative course of antibiotics. Doxycycline is often used against spirochaetes.

SNAP Tests are available to aid in diagnosis although currently they do not differentiate between having had the disease prior or having an active case.

Vaccinate for Lyme if it is a problem in your area. The vaccination of dogs for Lyme disease is a hotly debated issue among veterinarians.

The USDA approved an oral vaccine for wildlife in the spring of 2023. The vaccine, called "Borrelia Burgdorferi Bacterin," is spray-coated onto pellets that are meant to be consumed by white-footed mice. A vaccinated mouse will develop antibodies and should not be able to transmit the disease to other animals. Many states require the reporting of any diagnosed Lyme Disease cases.

"Doktor Schnabel von Rom" ("Doctor Beak from Rome"), engraving, Rome 1656. Physician attire for protection from the Bubonic plague or Black death.

Plague

*** Zoonotic

Yes, that plague as in the Middle Ages. However, what you probably didn't learn in high school history class is that it also killed hundreds of thousands of animals. Domestic livestock was affected causing food shortages and in the case of sheep deaths caused a wool shortage. Both domestic and wild felines died in great numbers unfortunately exacerbating the rodent/flea cycle.

There are several types of Plague. Historically Bubonic Plague was the killer in the Middle Ages. Pneumonic and septicemic are the others. All types are caused by the bacterium Yersinia pestis that lives in fleas. Exposure can also happen by inhalation of infectious respiratory droplets from people or pets with plague pneumonia.

Plague primarily affects wild rodents (woodrats, ground squirrels, mice, voles, tree squirrels and chipmunks) Rabbits and hares are sometimes affected. Cats and wild felines such as bobcats, lynx and mountain lions are also very susceptible. Canids seem to be less susceptible, but the disease has occurred in coyotes and foxes. Raptors and carnivores can transmit fleas and thus the disease. (AVMA)

Symptoms:

- Fever
- Enlarged lymph nodes
- Oral ulcers
- Diarrhea and Vomiting
- Low weight/Loss of weight
- Cough
- Discharge from eyes

Animals should be isolated immediately and caregivers wearing PPE. Control of fleas is critical, and intakes should always be inspected and given flea treatments.

Provide supportive care such as fluids. Plague is often treated with specific antibiotics from the aminoglycoside, fluoroquinolone and tetracycline families as well as antimicrobials. (AVMA) Work with your veterinarian. In some states you may need to make a report to public health officials.

Y. pestis does not survive for long periods outside a host. A household bleach solution, with a contact time of 30 minutes, should be used to decontamination the area.

Plague is still a very serious disease in humans and treatment should be sought immediately if symptoms appear.

Parvo

Parvo is another common disease that wildlife rehabilitators often see. The symptoms of parvo in wildlife can vary depending on the species and their physiological response to the virus. There are numerous strains of parvo that affect canids, felines, raccoon, skunk and mink.

Parvo is more common in young animals and those with a heavy worm load.

SNAP tests for canid Parvo are available through your veterinarian or veterinarian supply. Fecal and blood tests are also used.

Symptoms:

- Lethargy
- Fever
- Loss of appetite
- Diarrhea and vomiting
- Severe dehydration

These symptoms can be particularly severe in young animals, whose immune systems are not yet fully developed, making them more susceptible to the virus.

When a wildlife rehabilitator encounters a suspect case of parvo, several measures need to be taken to ensure the best possible outcome for the affected animal. The first step involves quarantining the animal to prevent any potential spread of the virus to other wildlife or domesticated animals. Quarantines need to last three to four weeks depending on the parvo strain.

Rehabilitators must follow strict biosecurity protocols to minimize the risk of cross-contamination. Use a bleach solution for cleaning.

Next, the rehabilitator will assess the animal's condition, taking note of its symptoms, physical appearance, and behavior. In suspected cases of parvo, a veterinarian may need to be involved for proper diagnosis through laboratory tests. Once a conclusive diagnosis is made, the rehabilitator will develop an appropriate treatment plan in collaboration with the veterinarian.

Treatment for parvo in wildlife typically involves supportive care to alleviate symptoms and provide the animal with the best chance of recovery. This can include intravenous fluids to combat dehydration, anti-nausea medication, antibiotics to prevent secondary infections, and medication to reduce gastrointestinal inflammation. These treatments aim to strengthen the animal's immune system and help combat the virus.

Additionally, rehabilitators must focus on creating optimal conditions for the infected animal's recovery. This may involve providing a quiet, stress-free environment, maintaining proper hygiene through frequent cleaning, and ensuring a nutritious diet to support the animal's weakened immune system. Regular monitoring of the animal's progress is essential to adjust the treatment plan as necessary.

There has been a definite intersection between Parvo and Distemper among domestic animals and wildlife. Several studies have been done on this. In their study, Caellaigh N. Kimpston et al., stated that "As humans and companion animals encroach on wildlife habitat, and as wildlife becomes increasingly urbanized, the potential for transmission between species increases. Ongoing monitoring of CPV and CDV in wildlife and increased efforts to vaccinate dogs and prevent spillover events are essential." (Kimpston, 2022)

Encouraging vaccination of domestic animals and keeping pets and wildlife separate is crucial.

Spring 2023 the USDA granted a "conditional license for the

first therapeutic solution to treat canine parvovirus. The Canine Parvovirus Monoclonal Antibody is a single, intravenous dose used to treat clinical signs caused by parvo in sick puppies and dogs, regardless of vaccination status". (AVMA).

Pox Virus

Often referred to as Squirrel Pox, it also affects chipmunks, rabbits, and groundhogs. There are also strains of pox viruses that affect marine mammals and birds.

Squirrel pox virus, also known as squirrel fibroma virus, is a viral infection that affects various species of squirrels. It belongs to the poxvirus family and is primarily transmitted spread by mosquitos, ticks, and lice. This affects red, grey, and fox squirrels.

Squirrel pox virus manifests as skin lesions or tumors, usually found around the eyes, mouth, and genitals of the affected squirrels. These growths can cause significant discomfort and may interfere with the squirrel's ability to eat, see, or reproduce.

Symptoms:

- Lesions
- Diarrhea and vomiting
- Discharge from eyes and nose

Keep animals in isolation while they have active lesions. The lesions aren't contagious, but they are painful and uncomfortable. So, give them soft blankets to lay on.

Currently, there is no known cure for squirrel fibroma virus. The viral infection can be challenging to treat due to its complex nature and the lack of specific antiviral medications that seem to work well.

Start by treating for fleas and ticks as they are carriers.

Treatment for squirrels infected with squirrel fibroma virus typically focuses on supportive care and symptom management.

This may involve providing proper nutrition, hydration, and creating a comfortable environment for the infected squirrel.

Healthy squirrels in a soft release. Photo credit: Ame Vanorio

Medication to alleviate pain, control secondary infections, or boost the squirrel's immune system may be necessary. Benadryl may help alleviate itching and some rehabbers have had positive results using herbal immune boosting remedies. L-lysine and vitamin B complex may help.

However, it is important to note that the outcomes for squirrels with squirrel fibroma virus can vary. The severity of the infection and the overall health of the individual squirrel play significant roles in the outcome. In cases where the virus has progressed significantly or caused significant debilitation, the chances of successful recovery may be limited.

Red squirrels in the United Kingdom are very susceptible to this virus. Grey squirrels in both America and Europe are often carriers but can and do get the disease as well.

Wear disposable gloves and a mask when handling the infected squirrel to minimize the risk of transmission. Thoroughly wash your hands before and after each interaction.

While the virus is not zoonotic it can live in the environment, and you want to reduce the risk of infections.

Rabies

***Zoonotic Disease with no cure

There are many strains of rabies which are tracked by the Center of Disease Control (CDC) to protect human health.

Many states have rabies vector species lists depending on what variants they have seen. Bat, Coyote, Fox, Raccoon, Skunk are the most common. Some states have restrictions on rehabilitation services for rabies vector species.

Rabies is seldom seen in squirrels and opossums although it is possible. We will talk more about the opossum's unique role in rabies prevention in Volume 3.

Symptoms:

- Depressed
- Loss of fear
- Locomotion problems and paralysis
- Salivation
- Biting and attacking other animals (regardless of size)
- Biting at their own bodies
- Staggering or circling
- Seizures

It's important to note that we don't always see that vicious "rabid" expression or behavior that characterizes rabies.

Currently, there is no known cure for rabies once symptoms appear. Rabies is a viral disease that affects the central nervous system and is almost always fatal once clinical signs develop. That is why prevention is crucial, and immediate medical attention should be sought if someone is bitten by an animal suspected of having rabies.

Raccoon with that stereotypical "rabid" look.

However, there are preventive measures available, such as post-exposure prophylaxis (PEP), which includes a series of vaccinations and, in some cases, administration of rabies immunoglobulin. This treatment can be highly effective in preventing the onset of rabies if administered promptly after exposure.

Prevention of rabies primarily revolves around vaccination. Vaccinating domestic animals, such as dogs and cats, is essential in controlling the spread of the virus. Additionally, avoiding contact with wildlife, especially animals displaying unusual behavior, is crucial to minimize the risk of exposure.

It is important to note that rabies is a serious and potentially deadly disease, and any suspicion of exposure or infection should be taken seriously. If you suspect you or someone else has been exposed to rabies, it is important to seek immediate medical attention from a healthcare professional or contact your local public health authority for guidance.

What is Pre-Exposure Rabies Prophylaxis?

Pre-exposure rabies prophylaxis (PREP) is a preventive measure undertaken before any potential exposure to the rabies virus. It involves a series of vaccinations that build immunity against the virus. By receiving the vaccine, wildlife rehabilitators can significantly reduce the likelihood of developing rabies if they are ever exposed to the virus. Completing the entire series is crucial for achieving the maximum protection that PREP offers.

As a wildlife rehabilitator, you work closely with wild animals, including those that could potentially be carriers of the rabies virus. By receiving PREP, you reduce the risk of contracting rabies if bitten or scratched by an infected animal. This protection provides peace of mind while handling potentially rabid wildlife.

Understanding Titer Checks:

A titer check, also known as a serologic test, measures the levels of antibodies in your bloodstream, specifically targeting the rabies virus. This test helps determine the effectiveness and persistence of your immune response following pre-exposure prophylaxis.

Through titer checks, you can evaluate your level of protection against rabies and make informed decisions about potential risks in your daily work. While pre-exposure prophylaxis provides a significant level of protection, everyone's immune response can vary. Regular monitoring ensures you are adequately protected and allows for any necessary adjustments to be made if your antibody levels decline over time.

The recommended frequency of titer checks for wildlife rehabilitators undergoing pre-exposure rabies prophylaxis may vary depending on individual circumstances and institutional guidelines. However, it is generally advised to have initial titer checks at 6-8 weeks after completing the vaccination series. Subsequent tests can be scheduled annually or biennially, depending on factors such as the intensity of your exposure to wildlife and any specific occupational health requirements.

Requirements:

States vary on their requirements for PREP. For instance, Kentucky "strongly recommends" getting your PREP. However, North Carolina makes it a condition to receive and maintain a license according to the Wildlife Rehabilitator of North Carolina.

Getting the Vaccine

I will say the first time I got my pre-exposure rabies prophylaxis I had to hunt it down! Apparently, the shots are quite expensive, and many health clinics and doctor's offices don't carry them. In addition, they are not normally covered by insurance.

I ended up driving an hour to a hospital and then getting it through their "travel" department. Since rabies is much higher in third world countries apparently missionaries and aid workers going to some poorer parts of the world get them.

Ringworm

***** Zoonotic**

Ringworm is a fungal disease that is zoonotic so wear PPE and cleanse enclosure thoroughly. Use bleach on laundry and enclosures.

What is Ringworm?

Contrary to its name, ringworm is not caused by a worm but by a group of fungi known as dermatophytes. These fungi can be found in the environment, such as soil, bedding, or grooming tools, and can infect both humans and animals.

Ringworm is highly contagious and can spread through direct contact or by sharing contaminated items.

Infected animals may develop circular patches of hair loss, which often appear scaly, crusty, or red. These patches may be itchy and may cause discomfort. However, it's worth noting that not all animals show symptoms, which makes it important to monitor and test exposed animals if ringworm is suspected.

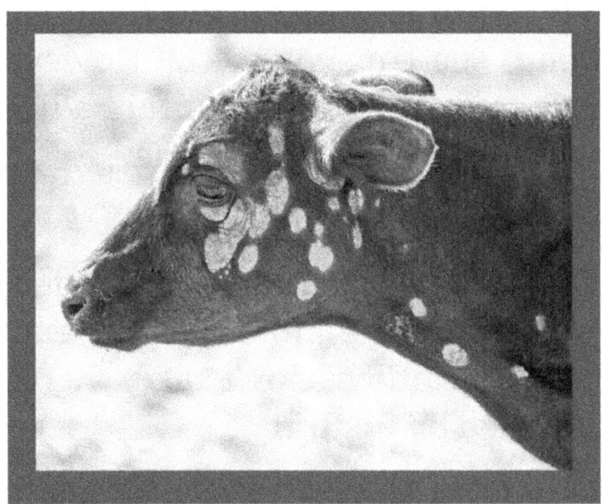

Calf with ringworm

Treatment of Ringworm

Treating ringworm on animals involves a combined approach of topical treatment and environmental control.

Here are the steps typically followed:

1. Isolation: To prevent the spread of ringworm, it is crucial to isolate the infected animal from others until treatment is complete. This prevents further contamination and transmission.

2. Topical Treatment with antifungal medications. Various antifungal creams and ointments are available and can be applied directly to the affected areas. The treatment duration can vary, but it typically lasts for several weeks or until the lesions are completely resolved.

Use caution with shampoos as they can spread the fungus to more areas.

My go to is to cleanse with Chlorhexidine and apply an anti-fungal cream. An over-the-counter inexpensive cream is good. It is also handy to have lime-sulfur dip on hand for various skin ailments.

3. Environmental Control: It is essential to thoroughly clean and disinfect the animal's environment to eliminate any remaining fungal spores. Regularly washing bedding, grooming tools, and toys in hot water and disinfectants is recommended. Vacuuming surfaces where spores can settle, such as carpets or upholstery, is also important. Kill the spores with a diluted chlorine bleach (1/4 c per gallon water).

4. Veterinary Care: Seek veterinary advice if the symptoms don't disappear in a couple of weeks. They may also suggest additional measures like systemic antifungal medications in severe or widespread cases.

Salmonella

*** Zoonotic

Salmonella, a notorious bacterium, is a major player in foodborne illnesses worldwide. Salmonella belongs to the Enterobacteriaceae family and is primarily divided into two species: Salmonella enterica and Salmonella bongori.

This pathogen can cause an array of symptoms, ranging from mild gastrointestinal discomfort to severe, life-threatening conditions. Salmonella infection, commonly known as salmonellosis, can occur when individuals consume contaminated food or come into contact with infected animals.

It is found in the intestines of diverse animals, including poultry, cattle, reptiles, and rodents. However, it is often associated with turtles and snakes.

Symptoms:

- Diarrhea
- Vomiting
- Abdominal pain
- Fever

Treatment primarily involves the management of symptoms through hydration and, in some cases, the use of antibiotics to combat severe cases or infection in vulnerable populations.

PPE should be worn when handling reptiles. Always wash your hands thoroughly with soap and water after handling turtles or cleaning their habitats. Regularly clean and disinfect turtle habitats, including tanks, aquariums, and any surfaces that come into contact with the animals or their waste. Avoid cleaning turtle habitats in kitchen or bathroom sinks to prevent cross-contamination.

Eastern Box Turtle. Photo by Ame Vanorio

Young children and elderly are susceptible so don't allow your children to handle reptile intakes. Young turtles with shells less than 4 inches (10.2 cm) in length are felt to be likely carriers.

Fecal cultures can determine if reptiles are carrying the bacteria. I have done this for educational reptiles as a precaution and also have people wash hands after a turtle encounter.

West Nile Encephalitis

*** Zoonotic

West Nile virus (WNV) is a viral disease that primarily affects birds but has the potential to impact various wildlife species including bats, horses, chipmunks, skunks, squirrels, and alligators.

WNV is primarily transmitted through the bite of infected

mosquitoes, which acquire the virus by feeding on infected birds. While some species have developed resistance to the virus, others, like bats and rodents, are prone to infection.

WNV affects a wide range of avian species, including songbirds, raptors, waterfowl, and others. corvids (crows, blue jays, and ravens) and raptors are the most susceptible However, it is important to note that not all infected birds show visible signs of illness, making it difficult to determine the true extent of the virus's impact on avian populations.

Symptoms:

- Inability to fly for birds
- Disorientation
- Lack of coordination
- Weakness
- Lethargy
- Tremors
- Seizures

Treatment

There is no specific treatment for West Nile virus and treatment consists primarily of supportive care.

Birds as Reservoir Hosts

Birds play a crucial role in the WNV transmission cycle. They act as amplifying hosts, allowing the virus to replicate in their bloodstream, which is then ingested by mosquitoes when they feed on infected birds. This cycle perpetuates the spread of the virus, making birds essential links in the transmission chain. Migratory birds, in particular, can facilitate the long-distance dissemination of

WNV, contributing to its wider distribution.

Ecological Implications

While it is known to infect humans and other mammals, its impact on wildlife populations is of particular concern. The impact of West Nile virus on wildlife is multifaceted and can have significant ecological implications. One of the major concerns is its potential to cause mortality in bird populations.

Large-scale die-offs of certain bird species have occurred in areas affected by the virus, resulting in disturbances to local ecosystems. These events can affect predator-prey relationships, disrupt pollination services, and alter the balance of various ecological processes.

Since bats are important contributors to ecological balance, their susceptibility to WNV warrants concern. Additionally, infected mammals may serve as amplifying hosts, allowing the virus to replicate and increase its transmission potential. This aspect of the disease cycle highlights the importance of understanding the role wild mammals play in the overall epidemiology of WNV.

The presence of WNV in wild mammals can have far-reaching consequences for ecosystems. As key components of food chains and ecological interactions, the illness's impact on these animals may disrupt trophic relationships and overall biodiversity. For example, a decline in bat populations due to WNV could lead to an increase in insect populations, potentially affecting vegetation and agricultural practices. Furthermore, the interconnectedness of species means that viruses can jump between mammals, birds, and humans. The health of wildlife populations directly influences human health, as zoonotic diseases can spill over into human populations.

Many diseases and parasite problems have common symptoms. It's not always possible right away to know the cause of the symptoms. You may need to wait to see a vet or for test results to come back.

Regardless of you can start treating many of these symptoms with common over the counter drugs.

Constipation

Constipation is when the animal can not rid themselves of feces. This is painful and can lead to infection or bloat.

Causes:

- Dehydration
- Lack of Food
- Inappropriate foods
- Stress

Dehydration is often the major cause that you will see with neonates, and this has a great effect on their digestive system. Rehydration is always the first step.

An enema of warm water can be helpful. Lubricate a small syringe and insert slightly inside the rectum. Water may squirt back out but that's ok.

If the animal has been in your care and develops constipation, consider that the formula is too concentrated or they need more genital stimulation to encourage peeing and pooping.

Some medications such as antihistamines can also cause constipation.

Probiotics

Pumpkin and applesauce are great sources of fiber that can help move bowels in an older baby. I am a big fan of feeding both as part of a balanced diet in the weaning and grow out phases as they are high in vitamins and antioxidants.

Lactulose (Generlac®, Constulose®, Enulose®) is a stool softener often used in cats with hairballs. Lactulose is available over the counter. It does not have a good flavor and some animals do not like the smell. Some veterinarian application add tuna or other flavors to encourage indigestion. This can be given orally or if easier placed on a paw for the animal to lick off.

Another drug recommended in Merck Veterinarian Manuel is bisacodyl (Dulcolax®) which is used off label since it is designed for humans. It's typically sold as tablets, suppositories, or enemas and not liquids so it can be a bit harder to administer on an active wild baby.

Diarrhea

Frequent loose and watery stools are one way the body tries to rid itself of pathogens. The stools may contain mucus or blood. Diarrhea can be painful and cause abdominal cramping.

Causes:

- Viral or bacterial illness
- Worms and protozoa
- Nursing on a dead mother
- Finder gives inappropriate foods
- Eaten something that causes allergy or poisoning

Diarrhea causes dehydration so the first step is always to give fluids. The next step would be to do a fecal examination and look for parasites and protozoans.

Remember there can be many reasons for diarrhea. For example, the animal may have roundworms but also a virus. Treat the worms and continue hydration protocol and then investigate the type of virus and what support the animal needs there.

You may need to treat an infection with antibiotics which may cause loose stools.

Probiotics are very helpful. Fox Valley, a formula company, has a LA-200 Probiotics for Digestive Health. They state that it helps balance the intestinal microflora during times of stress. Its easy to mix in with formula or fluids.

Bene-Bac Plus Prebiotic Pet Powder is another probiotic that I have used quite a bit. Bene Bac is over the counter, inexpensive and sold for pets. You can get it as a powder and a gel.

Kaolin Pectin (Kaopectolin®) is a human drug that is often used off-label by veterinarians. It is a liquid and can be given alone or mixed with food. Duravet has one developed for livestock. Remember these medications treat the symptoms not the cause.

Diarrhea In Rehabilitation:

The wildlife rehabilitator can also cause diarrhea. Feeding steps must be taken slowly so not to upset the baby's digestive track.

Causes of diarrhea within center include:

- overfeeding
- feeding too much too soon
- introduction of formula or new foods
- having an unclean area to prepare formula or using unclean equipment

Know what normal stool looks like for each species. Some species like cows in livestock or weasels in wildlife have naturally loose stools.

Pain is a real part of disease, parasites and just illness in general. I got a pretty bad case of COVID before the vaccine was available. During baby season and we all went under lockdown. I was so miserable but I had a barn full of precious tiny lives depending on me. And I realized my pain management regime for my wildlife was just not good enough.

As a human adult I at least knew what was going on (kinda, maybe, sorta) but these small animals did not. Add being stressed and scared to their pain.

In addition, as wildlife rehabilitators pain management is often not supported by our regulating agency. The Department of Fish and Wildlife and the Department of Natural Resources often say ***"Let Nature take its course"*** which is of course an incredibly uncompassionate and cruel thing to say. If they had an ounce of empathy, they would have outlawed trapping years ago.

Pain interferes with healing. Our goal is for them to heal and be able to be released. It makes good business sense to do this affectively and efficiently.

Symptoms of animals in pain are going to vary greatly and depend on the source of the pain. Some examples are:

- Pacing or the opposite refusing to move
- Agitation
- Holding body in abnormal way
- Not doing normal self-care behavior such as grooming
- May look drowsy or incoherent
- Vocalizing
- Chewing or biting objects including self
- Increased heart rate and pulse
- Sweating

One thing that stifles our ability to help our animals in pain is our inability to get pain medications. In today's world pain medication is a controlled substance and is thus under federal laws. Doctors and Veterinarians must keep close tabs on them.

Meloxicam (Metacam® Loxicom®) is a nonsteroidal anti-inflammatory drug (NSAID) that works well to reduce swelling and alleviate pain. In humans it's often used to treat arthritis. It is a prescription but is not a controlled substance. Vets are often open to letting rehabilitators keep it on hand. Felines are sensitive to NSAIDs so use caution there.

Butorphanol is a narcotic that works well and is well documented in animals including captive wildlife. It is however heavily regulated by the government, and I've heard vets say it can be a pain to get.

All animals feel pain. Unfortunately, medical literature on treating pain in reptiles and fish is pretty sparse.

DISEASE PREVENTION

Invariably, we bring in animals that carry diseases. Wildlife rehabilitation is about caring for sick, injured, and orphaned animals. Not the healthy one who is doing great out there in the wild.

If we look at the big picture, however, there are many things we can do to keep our animals healthy. Here is a list of non-vaccine things you should be doing to prevent disease.

- Work with your vet to develop an intake and treatment protocol.
- Keep wildlife separate from domestic animals.
- Have a quarantine area for incoming animals.
- Keep areas clean and sanitized.
- Always wear gloves and other PPE.
- Keep good records.
- Try to lower stress to improve health. (Yours and the animals!)

I am the first one to admit to feeling sad and squirmy when I go into a local animal shelter. I have been in bad ones, and I've been in good ones where the staff was just so amazing.

There is often the smell of disinfectant and the sterile nature of the cages. Keep in mind this is for the good of the group. Your local animal shelter is often a great resource for knowing how to keep animals and cages clean. Talk to them about their protocol.

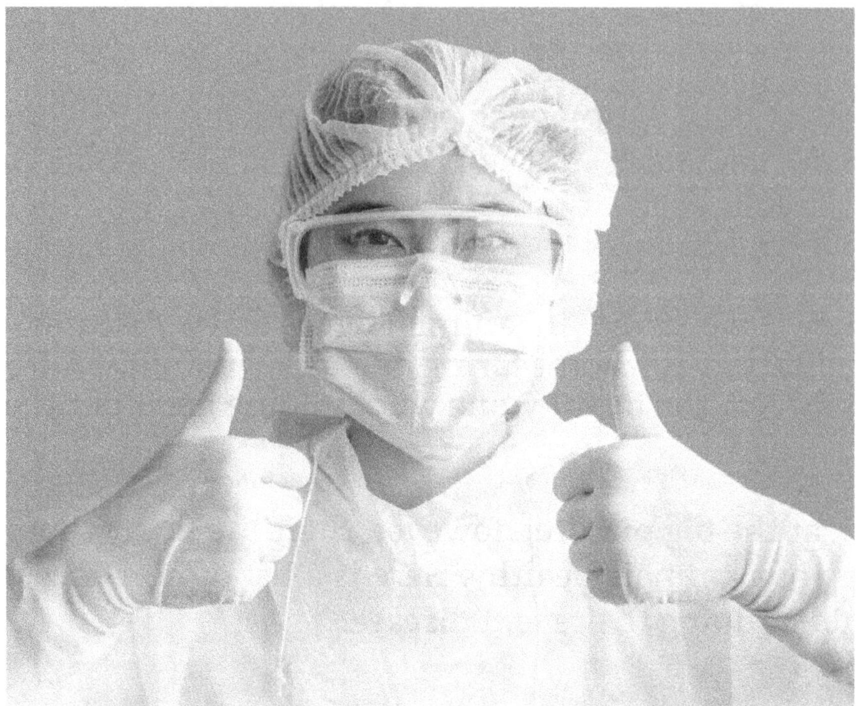

Vet Tech wearing Personal Protective Equipement (PPE)

What is PPE?

Personal Protective Equipment (PPE) refers to specialized equipment and clothing that is worn by individuals to minimize the risk of injury or illness in a hazardous environment. In the context of wildlife rehabilitation, PPE plays a crucial role in ensuring the safety and well-being of both the rehabilitators and the wildlife being treated.

PPE helps us to prioritize our safety and the safety of the animals. By wearing PPE such as gloves, masks, and goggles, rehabilitators can significantly reduce the chances of contracting diseases through direct contact or contaminated materials.

Do the best you can and don't beat yourself up. Supplies can get expensive so this is another thing to put on your Amazon list and explain how these things protect you and the critters.

PPE is also things like leather or other heavy duty gloves which minimize physical injuries. Wildlife, especially injured or frightened animals, may exhibit aggressive behaviors when approached by humans. At some point you will be bitten and scratched.

To safeguard against potential bites, scratches, or injuries, puncture-resistant gloves, sturdy footwear, and protective clothing. These measures provide essential physical barriers between the rehabilitator and the animal.

Maintaining Biosecurity: One fundamental principle of wildlife rehabilitation is maintaining biosecurity, which includes preventing the introduction or spread of diseases within rehabilitation centers. You don't want to bring in an animal with a serious disease and have it spread through your home or center. I have heard several stories where Parvo has done just that.

Along with disease control we want to talk about stress management. We all know that stress is in direct correlation to health – for animals and humans. Stress makes us more susceptible to illness.

Wild animals in captivity are stressed. Period.

Babies that are orphaned are stressed and afraid and depressed.

Ways to Manage Stress:

- Clean safe environment
- Quiet areas without a lot of human noise
- Nest boxes and hiding spaces.
- Socialization with similar aged or litter mates
- Environmental enrichment

The thing about having a neonate or young baby is the need to handle feeding, giving fluids, and administering pain meds. On top of that cages need to be cleaned and food and water dishes refilled.

One way is to try to bundle your chores. If the baby comes out for a feeding you can clean the cage and refill the water bottle. Obviously, a small infant needs frequent feeding but do what you can so there are no unnecessary interruptions between feedings.

Medication can often be hidden in food whether that's in a bottle or injected into a grape.

Keep in mind that reptiles and amphibians also feel stress. Turtles may refuse to leave shell and snakes may become agitated and strike.

Vaccines are used as one way to prevent diseases and their spread among populations. Young humans and domesticated animals get vaccinations on a regular basis. They are one tool we can use to prevent the spread of many diseases.

"An ounce of prevention is worth a pound of cure."

Benjamin Franklin said this over 300 years ago when talking about preventing house fires, but it's certainly applicable to disease prevention.

Why Vaccinate the Wildlife in Your Center?

Vaccination plays a critical role in safeguarding the health and well-being of the animals we support. I am unabashed in my support of vaccinating wildlife in my care but let's look at why and also the views from non-vaccination proponents.

OUTBREAK PROTECTION

The sad truth is anywhere we place animals in close proximity to one another there is a chance for disease to spread. We saw this happen with human populations during 2020 and the COVID pandemic.

One compelling reason to vaccinate wildlife is to prevent the spread of infectious diseases within our facility. As our rehabilitation center cares for a variety of species, animals from different backgrounds and habitats can come into close contact. This proximity increases the risk of disease transmission, which can have devastating consequences for the animals under our care. By vaccinating wildlife, we can significantly reduce the likelihood of disease outbreaks, protecting not only the individual animals but also the entire population within our facility.

Similarly, some species such as raccoons and deer may have large populations in your area. Wildlife biologists often use this reasoning to dissuade rehabilitation practice for "common" animals. However, the root problem is often a lack of or extinction of large predators. This is a whole other argument!

Centers have had highly contagious diseases such as distemper and parvo spread rapidly among young animals. Knowing what diseases are in your local wildlife populations is critical to developing a plan to help your animals.

In addition, keeping up with wildlife rehabilitation best practices through your local, state, or national group is advantageous.

Proponents of wildlife vaccination point to success stories such as the vaccination of raccoons against rabies in certain regions. This has helped control the spread of the disease and protect both wildlife populations and public health.

Vaccinating wildlife in rehabilitation can reduce the risk of disease transmission both within the rehabilitation facility and upon release into the wild. Diseases like rabies and distemper can have devastating impacts on wildlife populations, and vaccination can help mitigate these risks.

PROVIDES YOUR PATIENTS WITH IMMUNITY

Wildlife rehabilitation is all about saving an animal's life so that they may be released back into the wild.

The goal of immunization is to increase the animal's ability to fight the disease and to slow disease transmission among a population.

They keep the animal from suffering and increase their quality of life.

Furthermore, through vaccination, we contribute to the overall conservation efforts for many wildlife species. Vaccines have the potential to control and manage diseases that can devastate populations, especially those that are already endangered or vulnerable. By vaccinating wildlife, we play a vital role in protecting and preserving these precious species for future generations to enjoy.

Vaccinations ensure that individuals being moved or reintroduced are free from contagious diseases, minimizing the risk of disease outbreaks in new habitats, and promoting successful establishment and growth of reintroduced populations.

As wildlife rehabilitators, we have a lot invested in these animals. Time, energy, and money – often money from our own pockets. Not to mention sweat and tears.

COMMUNITY AND PUBLIC HEALTH

There is a lot to be said about the importance of public health. The act of wildlife rehab brings populations of animals and humans together.

Additionally, vaccinating wildlife enables us to mitigate the potential for zoonotic diseases to jump between animals and humans. As a rehabilitation center that interacts with wildlife, the risk of zoonotic disease transmission is a genuine concern.

By ensuring that the animals are vaccinated against common zoonotic and possibly dangerous diseases such as rabies we minimize the risk of any pathogens spreading to our staff or visitors, thus safeguarding public health.

Wildlife in today's world lives in close proximity to humans. Urban wildlife is on the rise. Vaccines have proven to be a way to manage and control many zoonotic diseases.

Cornell University advocates for wildlife vaccination to help control a number of zoonotic diseases including Rabies, Lyme disease and Bovine Tuberculosis. "Some diseases of wildlife can be transmitted to domestic livestock affecting the agricultural industry and human health. Bovine tuberculosis, caused by the bacteria Mycobacterium bovis, is an important veterinary health problem worldwide. The disease can be spread among cattle through coughing, particularly in crowded barns, and contaminated feed or watering sites."

White-tailed deer can transmit this disease as they interact with cattle in fields. Studies of oral vaccines using a weakened version of M. bovis have helped to reduce the infection rates in wildlife. (Abbott, 2022)

DISADVANTAGES OF VACCINES IN WILDLIFE

To be fair, there are several disadvantages to vaccination of wildlife in rehabilitation.

Probably the most cited disadvantage is the cost. Vaccines are expensive. In some states, including Kentucky, only a licensed veterinarian can administer the rabies vaccine. These costs can add up quickly especially if you have to pay a vet to come out an vaccinate.

In addition, juveniles can be hard to catch and handle to administer a vaccine. We do raise them to not want human contact!

Also, it should be noted, we often think of rabies vector species, as well as deer, and groundhogs, when planning to give immunizations. Many people who do squirrels and or bunnies do not vaccinate those species as they are not as high risk. However, that would geographically vary.

Some argue that vaccinating wildlife in rehabilitation raises ethical questions about interfering with natural selection and ecosystem dynamics. Vaccination may alter the immune system of wild animals, potentially affecting their ability to adapt and survive in their natural habitats.

One argument made by the Kentucky Department of Fish and Wildlife was that rehabbers were "holding" wildlife longer than they would otherwise because they were waiting to finish a vaccine schedule.

The debate surrounding the vaccination of wildlife in rehabilitation is complex, with valid arguments on both sides. While disease prevention, public health, and conservation efforts are key benefits, safety concerns, ethical considerations, and resource allocation present challenges.

Striking a balance between the benefits and risks requires careful evaluation and consideration of specific contexts, species, and disease dynamics. Continued research, collaboration between wildlife rehabilitators, veterinarians, and conservationists, and ethical discussions are necessary to inform evidence-based approaches to wildlife vaccination in rehabilitation.

VACCINATION SCHEDULES

Controversy also exists on how often and with what variant to vaccinate with. Raccoons and foxes can be tricky because both the canine and feline variants may be necessary.

What diseases you vaccinate for may also reflect your geographic location and what is present in your environment. For example. Distemper in wildlife is a big problem in my area. So, we feel distemper and rabies are the most important vaccines to give. To be clear we used the 5 way shot so Canine Distemper, Adenovirus Type 2 (CAV-2 cross protection CAV-1), Parainfluenza, and Parvovirus Vaccine (MLV) are all covered.

Vaccination schedules are somewhat arbitrary and often reflect older laws meant to contain diseases. There is little evidence that animals, including our beloved cats and dogs need annual boosters throughout their lives.

Studies have suggested that two shots lead to adequate antibodies. We give them boosters to make sure they are protected and to adhere to state regulations. For example, the rabies vaccine is legally required in the state of Kentucky for dogs, cats, and ferrets.

According to Merck's Veterinary Manual "Individual animal and vaccine variability make it difficult to estimate the duration of protective immunity."

Vaccines are not licensed for wildlife and there are few established administration schedules. Sadly, wildlife does not meet the need for funding for these studies. So, when we administer inoculations, it is with the understanding that it is "off label". More research is certainly needed in this area, not only for wildlife but as an assurance for quality public health.

Talk with your vet about what vaccine schedule to use. There are several good resources.

Karen Bailey founder of the Kentucky Wildlife Center presented a PowerPoint at the International Wildlife Conference in 2013 on Raccoon Rehabilitation: Infectious Disease Management. It contains a number of tips for best practices and gives her schedule for vaccinating raccoons.

Rabies used to be considered a public health threat in countries such as Germany and England. An aggressive program using trap/vaccinate/release and oral rabies vaccination (ORV) over the past twenty years has been very successful.

RABIES IN US WILDLIFE

According to the CDC, 92% of rabies cases came from wild animals. Specifically, bats, raccoons, skunks, and foxes, in descending order. The USDA works with the US Department of Fish and Wildlife to distribute rabies vaccines among wildlife populations in high-risk areas.

While Kentucky has not been considered a high-risk area, Oral Rabies Vaccination (OTR) has been dropped along the Virginia border to stop the spread of the raccoon variant more prevalent in the Appalachian Mountain region. Dr. Joanne Maki stated the goal is to "establish herd immunity within a rabies reservoir species. Doing so reduces virus transmission in wild animals, while also reducing the risk of rabies virus exposure in domestic species and humans".

Vaccines Have Been Critical In Saving Endangered Species

Another advantage to vaccinations is it helps species who are at risk due to low populations. With their limited numbers and reduced genetic diversity, endangered species are extremely vulnerable to outbreaks that can decimate their already struggling populations.

Vaccinations provide a key defense against these diseases, strengthening the immunity of individuals and protecting them from infection. By reducing the susceptibility to harmful pathogens, vaccines significantly contribute to preserving the health and well-being of endangered species.

Endangered animals have been saved by populations receiving immunizations. The Black-Footed Ferret is an example of an endangered species that recovered successfully in part due to a vaccination program.

The Black-Footed Ferret is susceptible to a variety of the plague they got from eating prairie dogs. In addition, distemper had lowered the population which was close to extinction. A controlled breeding program and vaccination schedule allowed the successful reintroduction of thousands of healthy ferrets in native prairie ecosystems.

In addition, due to the risk of mustelids to their population, the Black-Footed ferret has also been given the COVID vaccine.

While not a US species another notable example is the use of a vaccine in the successful eradication of canine distemper virus in the critically endangered Ethiopian wolf population. By immunizing domestic dogs, a potential reservoir of infection, and vaccinating wild wolves, researchers were able to control and ultimately eliminate the virus, thereby preventing the extinction of this unique species.

Vaccination of Wild Birds

On the other hand, opponents highlight cases where vaccination efforts have encountered challenges or unintended consequences. For instance, vaccinating wild birds against avian influenza has raised concerns about potential negative impacts on migratory patterns and interactions with non-vaccinated populations.

The critically endangered California condor (Gymnogyps californianus) began receiving vaccines against Avian flu this summer (Nature)

Avian flu, also known as avian influenza or bird flu, is a viral infection that primarily affects birds, both domestic and wild. It is caused by different strains of the influenza A virus, and certain strains can be highly contagious and cause severe illness and mortality in birds.

Wild birds, particularly waterfowl and migratory birds, serve as natural reservoirs for avian flu viruses. These birds can carry the virus without showing symptoms, enabling its spread across long distances during migration or through direct contact with other birds.

The transmission of avian flu to wild birds can occur through various routes, including direct contact with infected birds, ingestion of contaminated water or food, or exposure to contaminated environments. Infected birds shed the virus through respiratory secretions, feces, and other bodily fluids, facilitating its spread within bird populations.

Avian flu can have significant impacts on wild bird populations. Depending on the virulence of the virus and the susceptibility of bird species, the effects can range from mild illness to mass die-offs. Outbreaks of HPAI in wild bird populations have been reported in various parts of the world, resulting in significant ecological disruptions and mortality.

Avian flu is technically zoonotic. It has infected several domestic cats and at least one human in the US. Poultry raisers are worried about wild birds spreading the virus. The CDC states that 6,737 wild birds are affected and

Some poultry production farmers are against vaccination because they feel that it may amplify the disease. Vaccinated birds may continue to shed Avian flu thus infecting non-vaccinated birds.

EUTHANASIA

For wildlife rehabilitators, euthanasia means to end an animal's life, so they don't suffer or because their injuries are too severe for them to be able to live a quality life.

The word euthanasia comes from the Greek and means good death. Euthanasia should be quick and is meant to alleviate suffering.

As licensed wildlife rehabilitators our job is to release animals back into the wild to live the life they were intended to live. That means they need to be in good health, have use of their limbs, good vision, and be able to forage or catch prey.

If the animal is not able to recover and live naturally then it's our job to humanly euthanize them.

Understandably this is a hard topic to discuss and may result in you feeling sad. Know that I feel sad too writing this.

ESTABLISH PROTOCOLS

By establishing protocols, you put in set standards that you will follow prior to euthanasia. For larger centers, this may involve certain leaders. If you are a home center the decision may rest on one person.

Such policies may include animals that are in need of immediate euthanasia and animals that you will treat and then make a call. It's important to have timetables in place.

How long will you give the animal to make a significant recovery? I tend to err on giving a long recovery and in that time getting attached to the animal.

IMMEDIATE CASES MAY INCLUDE:

- An animal that meets the definition of a serious zoonotic disease such as rabies.
- An animal that is severely crushed by a car or maimed
- An animal that is actively dying

WAIT AND SEE CASES

For many animals, we need to give them time to respond to medical treatment. Some animals don't respond. We have all had animals who initially respond well and then pass and we wonder why.

You have also had cases, I'm sure where the animal does not make a complete recovery but is still able to live a full life.

TRAINING

For many centers, your veterinarian may perform your euthanasia's. This may be easier emotionally for the staff.

I personally use my vet because it's emotionally easier, even if I assist. Also, the vet has access to drugs which makes the process go smoother. My alternative is using a gun and I am not comfortable shooting animals.

If your center takes in a large number of animals, this may not be realistic cost-wise.

Some states have mandatory training that is required before a non-veterinarian can perform euthanasia. Persons may be required to hold Certification as a Euthanasia Technician (CET) to perform euthanasia.

You can earn a CET at a variety of institutions. The classes are open to anyone working with animals. Your state may have approved places where you can earn the CET.

CRITERIA

While there is no ideal form of euthanasia, the procedure you choose should attempt to meet the following criteria:

- Speedy loss of consciousness and death

- Easy and safe to administer

- Causes minimal psychological stress to the animal and to human observers

- Does not involve abuse by humans towards animal

- Doesn't damage tissues that would affect a necropsy ie: rabies and brain

This list comes from <u>The Minimum Standards Handbook</u> put together by International Wildlife Rehabilitation Council (see Resources).

THE GREY AREA

Sometimes an animal falls in that gray area. We are not sure if they will make a good recovery.

In that case, we need to think ahead and know what our options will be if the animal is not able to be released.

Education Animals

In some cases, the disabled animal may be able to become an educational animal. Educational animals are un-releasable wildlife that is used to educate the public.

Most education animals require additional permits from either the state or federal governments. They also require housing that meets certain specifications.

Not all wildlife requires a permit to be an education animal.

Depending on their species they may be allowed as a pet in your state or may not be considered a native regulated species in your state. Check your states laws.

Another question to ask yourself is will you be able to place this animal. The International Wildlife Rehabilitators has a placement board for un-releasable animals. Note that you must have proper permits to participate.

Some education animals may be easy to handle and travel to groups. Others may be display animals only.

CONSIDERATIONS OF EDUCATION ANIMALS

Must be a species that you can get a permit for or be able to place with another rehabber, park, or environmental education facility.

- Will the animal be free from pain
- Will the animal be able to have a quality life even with a disability
- How does the animal react to being around people – are they stressed and scared? Even a display animal needs to be able to not feel anxiety when people are viewing them.

Cons Education Animals?

Having education animals is a commitment. Most states require the animal to participate in education programs for the public a minimum number of times a year.

In addition, just like your pets, you need to consider a long-term plan for the animals. I am 58 years old and have two turtles that will probably outlive me.

In situations like that you need a plan for their care after your death. My will has a section for the turtle's care, and I have communicated this with my son. In the meantime, they need proper housing and care.

EMOTIONAL INTERFERENCE

Euthanasia decisions are hard. I am the first to admit I have emotional interference. I sometimes have a hard time making this decision because I WANT to help the animal.

That's why I became a wildlife rehabilitator. I want to help animals.

However, sometimes the helpful thing to do is euthanasia.

If you are faced with a hard decision, consult another rehabber who you know personally and trust or your veterinarian.

I would not recommend asking on the internet. Things like Facebook groups are full of bullies who don't understand your situation or are just very emotionally manipulative.

DEATH DOES NOT MEAN YOU HAVE FAILED

Death does not mean you have failed. You have helped the animal pass over humanely. They are at peace.

I know of many rehabbers who say a prayer as the animal passes. Do what feels right for you.

ACCEPTABLE MEANS OF EUTHANASIA

There are several ways you can use to euthanize an animal in your care. The way you choose may take into consideration the size of the animal. It may also consider your budget and what is available to you.

See Chapter 7 of Minimal Standards for a complete listing or simply discuss with your veterinarian. (IWRC)

DRUGS

Drugs such as barbiturates, typically combined with a sedative. Most states have strict rules on having access to "controlled substances" and require training, record keeping, and locked storage.

This method may only be available to a veterinarian or vet tech, depending on your state.

GUN

Gun Shot is considered an acceptable way to end an animal's life. While this may seem violent, if done properly it is quick.

Keep in mind that the person doing the shooting needs to be experienced in handling the weapon and understands safe practices.

PENETRATING CAPTIVE BOLT

Quick-acting, a bolt is fired into the skull. This is recommended for larger animals.

Requires special equipment, training, and a permit.

UNACCEPTABLE WAYS TO EUTHANIZE

There are many unacceptable ways to perform euthanasia. They are not permitted because they incur prolonged death and stress in the animal.

This is the list from the Minimum Standards Guide Chapter 7 of unacceptable methods:

- Acetone
- Air embolism
- Cyanide
- Drowning
- Electrocution
- Freezing
- Kill traps

And on a personal rage platform I just want to point out that several of these unacceptable methods and other inhumane methods are used in hunting, trapping and by farmers. With the full support of DNR and USFW and our tax dollars.

DISPOSAL OF BODY

After euthanasia, an exam should take place to make sure the animal is dead. Listening for a heartbeat with a stethoscope and checking for a pulse.

You can then follow your center's methods for disposal of the wildlife. Some local health departments require the body to be placed in the trash collection and some permit on-site burial.

Incineration is also an option. You may have access to an incinerator at a local animal control shelter.

When burying a carcass make sure it is deep enough not to be dug up by other animals. Dust lime over the body to help discourage any disease organisms.

Endangered animals and especially eagles have to be meet certain guidelines for disposal. Eagles, both bald and golden, bodies and feathers must be sent to the National Eagle and Wildlife Property Repository.

NECROPSY

A rehabilitator may choose to necropsy the carcass to learn more about why the animal died. They can do this at their facility or send the animal's body to a professional laboratory.

DONATION OF BODY

It is allowed to transfer a body to a museum, environmental education center or another licensed institution to be mounted for educational display. You may consider contacting such places before your baby season begins to see if they have any interest in specific species.

RESOURCES:

Abbott, Rachel (2020) Wildlife Vaccination - Growing in Feasibility? Cornell Wildlife Health Lab. https://cwhl.vet.cornell.edu/article/wildlife-vaccination-growing-feasibility

America Veterinary Medical Association (AVMA) has a great website with lots of resources however some information is behind an expensive membership wall. https://www.avma.org/

Bailey, Karen (2012) Raccoon Rehabilitation: Infectious Disease Management Presentation by Karen Baily at the International Wildlife Rehabilitation Council Conference 2012 available on pdf http://theiwrc.org/wp-content/uploads/2012/02/IWRC-Raccoon-Infectious-Disease-2012-handout-2-slides-per-page.pdf

Cornell Wildlife Health Lab has some great information and resources on their website. https://cwhl.vet.cornell.edu/

Hines, Ron DVM, PhD. Vetspace Website has some good articles on using medications with wildlife. https://vetspace.2ndchance.info/

Hotline for Wildlife (2018) Treating Sarcoptic Mange In Red Foxes https://hotlineforwildlife.org/wp-content/uploads/2018/11/Treating-Sarcoptic-Mange-in-Red-foxes.pdf

Kimpston, Caellaigh N. Hatke, Amanda L. Castelli, Benjamin et al (2022) High Prevalence of Antibodies against Canine Parvovirus and Canine Distemper Virus among Coyotes and Foxes from Pennsylvania: Implications for the Intersection of Companion Animals and Wildlife. American Society for Microbiology. https://journals.asm.org/doi/full/10.1128/spectrum.02532-21

Kozlov, Max (2023) US will vaccinate birds against avian flu for first time — what researchers think. Nature Magazine https://www.nature.com/articles/d41586-023-01760-0

Merck Veterinary Manual 2016 Eleventh Edition. I use both the print and the online version https://www.merckvetmanual.com/

Patrick Pearson, Connor Rich, Martin J.R. Feehan, Stephen S. Ditchkoff, and Stephen M. Rich (2023). White-Tailed Deer Serum Kills the Lyme Disease Spirochete, Borrelia burgdorferi, Vector-Borne and Zoonotic Diseases | doi:10.1089/vbz.2022.0095

Sapp SG, Rascoe LN, Wilkins PP, Handali S, Gray EB, Eberhard M, et al. Baylisascaris procyonis Roundworm Seroprevalence among Wildlife Rehabilitators, United States and Canada, 2012-2015. Emerg Infect Dis. 2016 Dec;22(12):2128-2131. doi: 10.3201/eid2212.160467 https://www.ncbi.nlm.nih.gov/pmc/articles/PMC5189140/

Sapp SGH, Gupta P, Martin MK, Murray MH, Niedringhaus KD, Pfaff MA, Yabsley MJ. Beyond the raccoon roundworm: The natural history of non-raccoon Baylisascaris species in the New World. Int J Parasitol Parasites Wildl. 2017 Apr 30;6(2):85-99. doi: 10.1016/j.ijppaw.2017.04.003 https://pubmed.ncbi.nlm.nih.gov/28529879/

Ame Vanorio is an organic farmer, environmental educator, and wildlife rehabilitator. She was raised on a traditional Kentucky farm with horses, cattle, and tobacco. Ame's hands on experience includes:

- 29 years of off-grid self-sufficient lifestyle experience

- 6 years urban homesteading

- Organizing and selling at Farmers Markets, Farm Stands, and CSA

- 15 years in wildlife conservation and licensed rehabilitation work

- 20 years in education

She holds graduate degrees in Education and Environmental Science and is the Founder/director of Fox Run Environmental Education Center.

Fox Run EEC is a non-profit that teaches environmental education, organic agriculture, and wildlife conservation. Ame is a licensed wildlife rehabilitator and teaches classes in the community and online.

Ame recently moved from Kentucky to Wisconsin to be closer to her son and family. She is focusing more on education projects and helping underserved communities experience nature and gardening.

You can follow us on Facebook and YouTube. Check out my Author Page on Amazon.

Thank you so much for reading and your support!! If you have found this book helpful please leave me a review on Amazon.

Ame and Friend